T0283342

The Sources
of Renewed
National Dynamism

MICHAEL J. MAZARR, TIM SWEIJS, DANIEL TAPIA

Prepared for the Office of the Secretary of Defense Office of
Net Assessment
Approved for public release; distribution is unlimited

NATIONAL SECURITY RESEARCH DIVISION

For more information on this publication, visit **www.rand.org/t/RRA2611-3**.

About RAND

RAND is a research organization that develops solutions to public policy challenges to help make communities throughout the world safer and more secure, healthier and more prosperous. RAND is nonprofit, nonpartisan, and committed to the public interest. To learn more about RAND, visit www.rand.org.

Research Integrity

Our mission to help improve policy and decisionmaking through research and analysis is enabled through our core values of quality and objectivity and our unwavering commitment to the highest level of integrity and ethical behavior. To help ensure our research and analysis are rigorous, objective, and nonpartisan, we subject our research publications to a robust and exacting quality-assurance process; avoid both the appearance and reality of financial and other conflicts of interest through staff training, project screening, and a policy of mandatory disclosure; and pursue transparency in our research engagements through our commitment to the open publication of our research findings and recommendations, disclosure of the source of funding of published research, and policies to ensure intellectual independence. For more information, visit www.rand.org/about/research-integrity.

RAND's publications do not necessarily reflect the opinions of its research clients and sponsors.

Published by the RAND Corporation, Santa Monica, Calif.
© 2024 RAND Corporation
RAND® is a registered trademark.

Library of Congress Cataloging-in-Publication Data is available for this publication.
ISBN: 978-1-9774-1325-3

Cover: Summit Art Creations/Adobe Stock.

Limited Print and Electronic Distribution Rights

This publication and trademark(s) contained herein are protected by law. This representation of RAND intellectual property is provided for noncommercial use only. Unauthorized posting of this publication online is prohibited; linking directly to its webpage on rand.org is encouraged. Permission is required from RAND to reproduce, or reuse in another form, any of its research products for commercial purposes. For information on reprint and reuse permissions, please visit www.rand.org/pubs/permissions.

About This Report

This report is part of a larger project that considers the societal sources of national dynamism and competitive advantage. The authors examine the ways in which national dynamism can be renewed—how great powers that begin to stagnate or even decline can recapture energy and competitive advantage. They do so by using historical evidence to develop typologies for the causes of national decline, pathways and processes of national renewal, and distinct national strategies that produce renewal. The report concludes by drawing lessons from this historical evidence for U.S. strategy.

RAND National Security Research Division

This research was sponsored by the Office of Net Assessment within the Office of the Secretary of Defense and conducted within the International Security and Defense Policy Program of the RAND National Security Research Division (NSRD), which operates the National Defense Research Institute (NDRI), a federally funded research and development center sponsored by the Office of the Secretary of Defense, the Joint Staff, the Unified Combatant Commands, the Navy, the Marine Corps, the defense agencies, and the defense intelligence enterprise.

For more information on the RAND International Security and Defense Policy Program, see www.rand.org/nsrd/isdp or contact the director (contact information is provided on the webpage).

Acknowledgments

This report represents the views of the authors and is partly informed by a wide variety of RAND work on the future of international order and strategic competition. The authors would like to thank James Baker and the staff of the Office of Net Assessment for supporting the research, Jim Mitre of the RAND International Security and Defense Policy Program for his assistance, Eline de Jong and Abe de Ruijter at the Hague Centre for Strategic

Studies for their research assistance, and Bryan Frederick and James Gold-geier for their thoughtful and helpful reviews.

Summary

History is full of great powers that hit their peak of competitive power and then stagnate and eventually decline. There are fewer cases of great powers that have confronted such headwinds and managed to generate a repeated upward trajectory—to renew their power and standing in both absolute and relative terms. Arguably, that is precisely the challenge that faces the United States. Its competitive position is threatened both from within (in terms of slowing productivity growth, an aging population, a polarized political system, and an increasingly corrupted information environment) and outside (in terms of a rising direct challenge from China and declining deference to U.S. power from dozens of developing nations). Left unchecked, these trends will threaten domestic and international sources of competitive standing, thus accelerating what is—at the time of writing—the relative decline in U.S. standing.

Issue

In this report, we seek to shed light on this challenge by examining the problem of national decline and renewal. It is part of a larger study on the societal determinants of a nation's competitive position, which has nominated several key qualities that determine a society's competitive success and failure. The findings of the first phase of the study suggest that it is very difficult for countries to achieve multiple periods of efflorescence or national peak dynamism. This report is one of several independent second-phase analyses on distinct topics that examine the prospects for the United States to do so, combining historical case analysis with contemporary assessments.

Approach

In this analysis, we were primarily—but not solely—interested in nations that have traditionally been characterized as *great powers*, which are typically defined as states that hold a predominant or coleading position in one region, that both have and are recognized to have significant influence in world politics (including the projection of military force), and that have been able to maintain or renew their position in world politics for a significant period. In some instances, our analysis includes nations that no longer fall into this category, such as the Netherlands and Great Britain, but which once sat at the top of global hierarchies. Their subsequent transformation into less dominant but wealthy—and by many measures successful—societies tells an important story.[1] However, we have not included processes or projects of national renewal in much smaller or less strategically significant nations, even though their assessment could supply potentially interesting lessons.

Key Findings

- *Recovery from significant long-term national decline is rare and difficult to detect in the historical record.* When great powers have slid from a position of preeminence or leadership because of domestic factors, they seldom reversed this trend. Some cases of partial decline do not appear to be a comprehensive national fall because there was a timely and successful process of anticipatory renewal.
- *The United States may be entering a period requiring the kind of anticipatory national renewal that we found in several historical cases.* In Britain and the United States (and likely in other cases that we did not review in depth), societies identified challenges to their dynamism and competitive position and undertook broad-based social, political, and economic reforms to sustain their power. They had not yet declined significantly (if at all) when these processes began, and it is not clear how severely their competitiveness would have otherwise suffered. However, the risk of more rapid decline was clear, and the reform and renewal efforts very likely underwrote continued relative power for decades if not longer.
- *Several common factors appear to distinguish cases of successful anticipatory renewal from failures.* As noted above, we assessed the histor-

---

[1]   For an extensive catalog of the ways in which British dynamism has declined, see Resolution Foundation and the Centre for Economic Performance, London School of Economics, *Ending Stagnation: A New Economic Strategy for Britain*, Resolution Foundation, December 2023, especially pp. 1–94.

ical record and our three primary cases in light of our preliminary research and the seven major societal characteristics associated with competitive success.

- *The United States does not yet appear to be demonstrating widespread shared recognition of societal challenges or determination to reform and change in key issue areas.* In this sense, it has not yet reached the position of Britain in the 1840s and 1850s or the United States after the 1890s, at which times both nations witnessed a surge of generalized reform to address multiple social challenges that resulted in broad-based national renewal. The United States does not yet have a shared recognition of the problem: Although some challenges are generating widespread frustration, there is no emerging consensus on the barriers to renewal that demand urgent action. The essential problem is seen in starkly different terms by different segments of society and groups of political leaders. This creates a distinct challenge for the multiple efforts to solve key issues, which is a typical hallmark of periods of national renewal: As a result, opportunity may not emerge.

- *The United States has all the preconditions for a potential agenda of anticipatory renewal.* It is not consigned by international politics to further relative decline, especially regarding China (which has its own problems in this regard). The United States is not in the position of the Soviet Union in the 1980s. It has tremendous residual strengths and a proven capacity for resilience and renewal. It has the scale and the industrial and scientific foundations to remain one of the great powers at the apex of world politics. It has a rich reservoir of social actors capable of conducting the same sort of campaign for reform and renewal that occurred in Victorian-era Britain and the turn-of-the-20th-century United States.

Contents

About This Report iii
Summary v
Figures and Tables xi

CHAPTER 1
The Challenge of National Revitalization 1

CHAPTER 2
Defining National Decline and Renewal: A Limited Set of Cases 9
Examples of Renewal: Qualitative Cases 10
Quantitative Indicators of Decline and Renewal 15

CHAPTER 3
A Modified Concept: Anticipatory Renewal 21

CHAPTER 4
Sources of National Decline and Stagnation: A Review of the
    Literature 27
Factors Identified in the First Phase of Research 27
Classic Challenges to Great Powers: The Literature on National
    Decline 29
More-Extreme Examples: The Literature on Societal Collapse 37
Summary: Factors Associated with National Decline 39

CHAPTER 5
Case Studies of National Renewal: Essential Narratives 41
Victorian-Era Britain 43
Post–Gilded Age United States 44
Late–Cold War Soviet Union 46

CHAPTER 6
Characteristics Associated with National Renewal 51
A Clear Recognition of Key Problems 52
Accurate Diagnosis of the Challenges 55

A Problem-Solving Mindset 55
Multiple and Overlapping Efforts to Solve Distinct Challenges 58
Capable Governance Structures and Social Institutions 60
Elite Commitment to the Common Good.................................... 60
Participation in an Era's Core Model of Value Creation.................... 62
Sustainable Access to Essential Resources for Renewal (Financial and
    Material) 63

CHAPTER 7
Lessons for the United States 65

APPENDIXES
A. Case Study: Victorian-Era Great Britain................................. 71
B. Case Study: Post-Gilded Age United States 83
C. Case Study: Late-Cold War Soviet Union................................ 93

References 105

Figures and Tables

Figures

1.1. World GDP Growth over Two Millennia..........................7
2.1. Relative Standing of the Great Powers............................16
2.2. Leading States in the International System, 1980–2012,
     Using Global Power Index...17
2.3. GDP Per Capita, Selected Great Powers, 1500–1900..............18
2.4. Permanent Productivity Growth in Britain........................19

Tables

1.1. Outcome Indicators—Factors to Measure Competitive
     Success 4
2.1. Cases of National Rise, Decline, and Potential Renewal.........11
3.1. Causal Links: Anticipated Decline and National Competitive
     Position...24
4.1. Selected Theories of Societal Decline.............................30
5.1. Addressing Sources of National Decline: Britain in the
     Victorian Era..45
5.2. Addressing Sources of National Decline: Post–Gilded Age
     United States 47
5.3. Addressing Sources of National Decline: Late–Cold War
     Soviet Union...48
7.1. Comparing Attributes of Anticipatory Renewal Versus
     Decline 66
7.2. Requirements for National Renewal and the Current
     U.S. Case 68

CHAPTER 1

The Challenge of National Revitalization

History is full of great powers that hit their peak of competitive power and then stagnate and eventually decline. There are fewer cases of great powers that have confronted such headwinds and managed to generate a repeated upward trajectory—to renew their power and standing in both absolute and relative terms. Arguably, that is precisely the challenge that faces the United States. Its competitive position is threatened both from within (in terms of slowing productivity growth, an aging population, a polarized political system, and an increasingly corrupted information environment) and outside (in terms of a rising direct challenge from China and declining deference to U.S. power from dozens of developing nations). Left unchecked, these trends will threaten domestic and international sources of competitive standing, thus accelerating what is—at the time of writing—the relative decline in U.S. standing.

In this report, we seek to shed light on this challenge by examining the problem of national decline and renewal. It is part of a larger study on the societal determinants of a nation's competitive position,[1] which has nominated several key qualities that determine a society's competitive success and failure. The findings of the first phase of the study suggest that it is very difficult for countries to achieve multiple periods of efflorescence or national peak dynamism. This report is one of several independent second-phase analyses on distinct topics that examine the prospects for

---

[1] Michael J. Mazarr, *The Societal Foundations of National Competitiveness*, RAND Corporation, RR-A499-1, 2022.

the United States to do so, combining historical case analysis with contemporary assessments.

In this analysis, we were primarily—but not solely—interested in nations that have traditionally been characterized as *great powers*, which are typically defined as states that hold a predominant or coleading position in one region, that both have and are recognized to have significant influence in world politics (including the projection of military force), and that have been able to maintain or renew their position in world politics for a significant period. In some instances, our analysis includes nations that no longer fall into this category, such as the Netherlands and Great Britain, but which once sat at the top of global hierarchies. Their subsequent transformation into less dominant but wealthy—and by many measures successful—societies tells an important story.[2] However, we have not included processes or projects of national renewal in much smaller or less strategically significant nations even though their assessment could supply potentially interesting lessons.

It is worth keeping in mind that national renewal has meant something different to such countries as the Netherlands and Great Britain (and even to countries with older histories of geopolitical greatness, such as Sweden) than to countries whose pure scale and economic or military heft have kept them in the great-power category. For formerly predominant powers who no longer aspire to anything like true great-power status, national renewal applies almost exclusively to domestic or absolute measures of success. This is an important model to consider, insofar as some advocates of U.S. retrenchment appear to have something similar in mind for a U.S. approach to renewal. Many of the essential requirements for national renewal, or the variables that produce or obstruct it, are common to great powers seeking restored predominance and middle powers desiring rejuvenated national dynamism in a humbler geopolitical sense. But our focus here is on great powers that have renewed their status as world leaders.

---

[2] For an extensive catalog of the ways in which British dynamism has declined, see Resolution Foundation and the Centre for Economic Performance, London School of Economics, *Ending Stagnation: A New Economic Strategy for Britain*, Resolution Foundation, December 2023, especially pp. 1–94.

In considering this version of national decline and renewal, we focused on measures of both absolute and relative power. In the first phase of the project, we developed a set of nine criteria to judge national competitive success and failure, incorporating both absolute and relative measures. We remain convinced that it is essential to include absolute measures of success because they often provide a critical window onto national dynamism and the sustainability of a nation's relative competitive position. At the same time, relative measures are essential because they capture a nation's comparative success and standing with regard to its peers. Table 1.1 lists these nine factors.

Assessing such a set of complex issues is methodologically challenging. Every prospective case involves a complex interaction of many variables in the following analytical focus areas: the nature of decline, the structure of renewal, and the viability of national strategies to promote it.[3] In examining these areas, we are very much in the analytical landscape described by John Lewis Gaddis in which a nonlinear, unpredictable mixture of factors makes it impossible to treat any cause as a truly independent variable.[4]

Such an assessment is also difficult because understanding renewal is not the same as understanding the sources of national development writ large. The qualities or choices that promoted a nation's first moves into economic development, technological dynamism, and competitive success might be different from the characteristics required for renewal once that initial energy begins to flag. The ebbing of a nation's basic qualities of competitive dynamism often produces decline and creates the need for renewal;

---

[3] For example, one study argues that a single case of national decline—the Han dynasty in China—was "a complicated affair that evolved across multiple temporal, social, political, economic, and environmental cycles and processes." However, these sorts of combinations—environmental pressures combined with demographic, economic, and social issues and a political inability to adapt—can be seen in other cases as well. See Tristram R. Kidder, Liu Haiwang, Michael J. Storozum, and Qin Zhen, "New Perspectives on the Collapse and Regeneration of the Han Dynasty," in Ronald K. Faulseit, *Beyond Collapse: Archaeological Perspectives on Resilience, Revitalization, and Transformation in Complex Societies*, Southern Illinois University Press, 2016, p. 87.

[4] John Lewis Gaddis, *The Landscape of History: How Historians Map the Past*, Oxford University Press, 2004.

TABLE 1.1

Outcome Indicators—Factors to Measure Competitive Success

Indicators of Competitive Success and Advantage	Historical and Current Examples and Metrics
Longevity in terms of long-term socioeconomic and geopolitical resilience that maintains national identity over an extended period and promotes extended cultural and social influence	• Trends in national power measures • Collapse or surrender of rival • Long-term, indirect, and diffuse social, cultural, or political influence
Sovereign ability to protect the safety and prosperity of citizens against capabilities or threats of other states, nonstate actors, and systemic risks	• Power to prevent large-scale territorial aggression against homeland • Ability to prevent harassment or disruption of society short of war
Geopolitical freedom of action in terms of the ability to make free and unconstrained sovereign decisions and to take actions in the international system to greatest degree relative power will allow	• Absence of coercive control by regional or global hegemon • Self-sufficiency in materials and factors necessary for freedom of action
Military advantage or dominance, locally or globally, and the ability to project power	• Global military dominance, either generally (e.g., Rome, post–Cold War United States) or in specific domains (e.g., British maritime dominance) • Ability to project power from a distance
Leadership of or membership in predominant alignments of military and geopolitical power	• Modern treaty-based alliances, multilateral or bilateral • Less formal security relationships
Predominant economic strength—globally, within a region, or within one or more industries	• Total or per capita gross domestic product (GDP) • Share of global trade, investment, or research in critical industries
Strong to predominant position in global trade, investment, and capital markets (relative to size of GDP and other factors)	• Role in regional or global trade networks (e.g., Egypt, Rome, Britain, the United States) • Dominance of national currency • Predominant power in economic institutions
Strong to predominant position in ideological and paradigmatic categories and global narratives and norms, attractive power, and international institutions and standards	• Cultural influence • Alignment with leading global norms and values • Leadership of international organizations and norm-setting processes

4

Table 1.1—Continued

Indicators of Competitive Success and Advantage	Historical and Current Examples and Metrics
Strong or leading position in frontier technology; leading or dominant role in key emerging industrial sectors	• Domestic capabilities and industries in leading industries of the era • Measures of relative technological standing • Proportion of research and development spending in key industries

SOURCE: Adapted from Mazarr, 2022, p. 18.

this tendency might be difficult to reverse merely by increasing the factors responsible for the country's success to that point.[5]

For this analysis, we relied primarily on reviews of history and theory. In the first phase of the study, we conducted extensive research into multiple literatures bearing on the question of national rise, decline, dynamism, and stagnation and analyzed their findings.[6] In this effort, we expanded on work done in that phase to more deeply examine the formal theories on national rise and fall. We reviewed a second major literature as well: studies on national or societal collapse and the substantial literature critiquing some of those analyses. In adjacent fields, we also looked at historical economic

[5] A good example may be one of the characteristics nominated in the first phase of this study: national ambition and will. An intense commitment to national development and achieving international status is a common ingredient in many stories of national rise. However, doubling down on that quality when confronted with stagnation can be counterproductive, producing more global reactions to the country's now-overweening ambitions and perhaps generating overreach. Something different and more nuanced is required to underwrite renewal.

[6] Mazarr, 2022.

studies of particular cases,[7] economic phenomena,[8] and general research in sociology and political science on power cycles,[9] and crisis and reform.[10]

Using that research, we identified a set of cases of great-power rise and decline, and from that set, we sought to identify cases of renewal. First, we reviewed the 12 cases examined in detail in the first phase of this study: ancient Rome, Song China, Renaissance Italy, 17th- and early-18th-century Sweden, imperial Spain, 18th- and 19th-century France, the Ottoman and Austro-Hungarian Empires, Meiji Japan, and the United States and Soviet Union of the 20th century.[11] Second, we examined the general literatures on national rise and decline and imperial collapse, basing our case selection on Paul Kennedy's seminal *Rise and Fall of the Great Powers*,[12] Jack Levy's *War in the Great Power System*,[13] and other publications. We reviewed the general trajectory of modern great powers from the 16th century onward and identified trends of decline and renewal.

One of the difficulties associated with comparisons across such extended timescales is that renewal before and after the industrial revolution has meant radically different things. Figure 1.1 shows the classic rapid growth or "hockey stick" pattern of economic growth over the past 2,000 years. The trajectory begins to pick up after 1500, accelerates around

---

[7] Carlos Álvarez-Nogal and Leandro Prados De La Escosura, "The Rise and Fall of Spain (1270–1850)," *Economic History Review*, Vol. 66, No. 1, February 2013.

[8] Robert B. Barsky and Luts Kilian, *A Monetary Explanation of the Great Stagflation of the 1970s*, National Bureau of Economic Research, Working Paper No. 7547, February 2000.

[9] William R. Thompson, "Dehio, Long Cycles, and the Geohistorical Context of Structural Transition," *World Politics*, Vol. 45, No. 1, 1992.

[10] Colin Hay, "Crisis and the Structural Transformation of the State: Interrogating the Process of Change," *British Journal of Politics and International Relations*, Vol. 1, No. 3, October 1999; Mounir Mahmalat and Declan Curran, "Do Crises Induce Reform? A Critical Review of Conception, Methodology and Empirical Evidence of the 'Crisis Hypothesis,'" *Journal of Economic Surveys*, Vol. 32, No. 3, 2018.

[11] Mazarr, 2022.

[12] Paul Kennedy, *The Rise and Fall of Great Powers: Economic Change and Military Conflict from 1500 to 2000*, Vintage, 1989.

[13] Jack Levy, *War in the Modern Great Power System: 1495–1975*, University Press of Kentucky, 1983.

FIGURE 1.1

World GDP Growth over Two Millennia

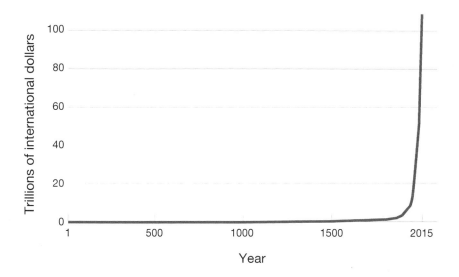

SOURCE: Adapted from Our World in Data, "Data Page: Global GDP over the Long Run," from Max Roser, Pablo Arriagada, Joe Hasell, Hannah Ritchie, and Esteban Ortiz-Ospina, "Economic Growth," webpage, 2023 (data adapted from World Bank, Bolt and van Zanden, and Angus Maddison's estimates). The *international dollar* is a hypothetical currency used to make comparisons of monetary indicators of living standards and are adjusted for inflation and differences in cost of living among countries.

1800, and shows stratospheric results in the centuries after that. National renewal before 1500 and after 1800 are simply different concepts. Before 1500, renewal had more of a quality of reconstitution to an established model or level of dynamism, which changed little (in terms of growth rates, technologies, and other important measures) for very long periods. (Many measures of technological development—especially such recent ones as computing power and network participation—show a similar hockey stick pattern.) In the industrial era and the emerging informational era, renewal demands keeping up with dramatic progress. For this reason, while we did consider older cases (not only ancient Rome but also comparative periods of flourishing and decline in Chinese history), our primary research focus was on modern cases.

We discovered very few cases of large-scale, generalized national revitalization as we define it here. We eventually settled on a modified focus of *anticipatory renewal,* cases in which great powers—formally and consciously or implicitly and in a grassroots manner—sensed a negative trajectory and took steps to prevent more serious decline before it occurred.

CHAPTER 2

Defining National Decline and Renewal: A Limited Set of Cases

The first step in our analysis was to provide more-specific understandings of the basic concepts or trajectories at the core of the analysis. The basic phenomenon we seek to assess is *national renewal*, which we define as reversing a trajectory of decline through some combination of inherent characteristics and intentional policy, which thus improves national standing in both absolute and relative measures. In our initial survey of the literature on the rise and fall of great powers, the challenge was just how few cases appear to meet that definition.

However, stories of renewal need not be as linear, comprehensive, or neat as our definition implies. The actual trajectories of nations are typically far more complex, which complicates the task of looking for decline and renewal cases. For example, some nations might sustain their military dominance as an echo of former greatness long after their economic, social, and technological trajectories have reversed. In some cases, a falling away from national rise can involve merely stagnation rather than stark decline— at least in some measures and at least for a time. A nation might enjoy a peak in relative power partly because other nations have declined or experienced temporary weakness, which happened to the United States after 1945. Relative standing is always a product of internal dynamism and the dynamics of the international system: Some competitive and dynamic nations have simply been caught or bypassed by other quickly rising nations, as has happened to the United States vis-à-vis China since the late 1970s.

As noted in Chapter 1, another distinction is between countries that have been renewed versus those that have been resurrected. Modern postwar reconstruction success stories—in Germany, Japan, South Korea, Poland,

and others—generally fall into the latter category. Their stories capture how new models of industrial development, often aided by importing technologies and techniques, are grafted onto reconstructed social and political traditions that existed before wartime devastation. We are interested in national decline and renewal that occur for reasons inherent to the nations themselves and their surrounding context, not cases of original development out of poverty or postwar recovery.

For this analysis, national renewal does not imply a simple response to a one-off crisis. Nations sometimes face mortal threats, including environmental disasters, lost battles, nonexistential expeditionary wars, plagues and pandemics, or invasion. Some respond vigorously and quickly recover their previous position; others do not. But such cases of running into momentary (if perilous) challenges are not the same as confronting the need for generalized reform to deal with a widespread collection of social challenges.

Examples of Renewal: Qualitative Cases

We examined two major sources of evidence for identifying possible cases of national renewal. The first was a general, qualitative review of historical evidence. Table 2.1 summarizes the cases reviewed for this analysis. In selecting cases, we mainly drew from the roster of modern great powers, with a particular emphasis on those that had experienced a significant rise or decline over an extended but still limited period (generally less than a century). We did not consider cases of renewal that occurred over many centuries or millennia because while certain territories might bear cultural and social continuities—and even the same name—they are politically distinct. For example, we do not consider China's post-1970 rise to be a renewal of its strength prior to 1700. Importantly, we did not seek a representative sample in any quantitative sense but rather interesting cases that could offer general lessons for the United States.

Of the cases we considered, several represent generalized decline. Several reflect industrial development–fueled rises. Only two cases in specific periods—Britain in the Victorian era and the United States from about 1870 through about the 1930s—represent what could be called a notable national

TABLE 2.1

Cases of National Rise, Decline, and Potential Renewal

Case	Rise or Decline Type	Primary Events and Characteristics
Great Britain	Industrial development; anticipatory renewal	Long period with leading global role; peak of power in mid- to late-19th century; relative decline and fragmentation of empire from 1940 through 1950s; challenges to postwar domestic dynamism, "British disease"; recurring efforts at national renewal, both early (19th century) and later (1970s recovery from stagnation)
United States	Industrial development; anticipatory renewal	Long rise as dominant industrial power; significant global leadership by early-20th century, dominant industrial democracy from 1940s, peak of power from 1989 to early 21st century; recovered from multiple earlier challenges, including 1870s–1920s social tensions; degree of decline at the time of writing is contested, but relative power (e.g., vis-à-vis China) has ebbed, and many domestic challenges create risk of anticipated decline
Netherlands	General geopolitical rise and relative decline; persistent national dynamism	Peak of power in 17th century with role as predominant maritime and financial power in Europe; post-17th century gradual decline, did not industrialize at the British pace; social and economic dynamism remains strong; not so much a case of national renewal as one of persistent energy and competitiveness in a smaller nation
Japan	Industrialization, recovery from war, incomplete effort at renewal from stagnation	Two major periods of rise or recovery: Meiji industrialization and post-1945 rebuilding (but neither may count as a national renewal as we define it); post-1980s efforts to escape economic stagnation represent an effort at national renewal
Prussia (Germany)	Industrialization, recovery from war; persistent national dynamism from the 19th century	Period of national unification leads to rise of unified and stronger Germany, which becomes a leading great power by the late-19th century and the Continent's dominant military power by the 1930s; German industrial power surpassed Britain's in some categories by the early 20th century; post-1945 it was not a major global great power; economic development and unification upgraded the country's relative strength but was not aimed at a position of global competition as a great power

Table 2.1—Continued

Case	Rise or Decline Type	Primary Events and Characteristics
Soviet Union (Russia)	Industrialization, failed effort to renew power 1980s–1990s	Long period of reliance on size and population as foundation for great-power status; intermittent efforts at modernization did not achieve significant results until 1920s–1960s, which helped fuel the rise of the Soviet Union (USSR) as a bipolar hegemon; gradual decay of the Soviet system produced stagnation and eventual collapse of empire and economic crisis in 1990s; despite expressions of power, no general post-1990s renewal
Habsburg Spain	General geopolitical rise and relative decline	Peak of power in second half of 16th century; decline from loss of imperial revenues, imperial overextension, lack of ability to align to demands of first industrial revolution, poor leadership, role of religious and political restraint and orthodoxy; some gradual sectoral renewal in 20th century but no generalized national power renewal
Austro-Hungarian Empire	General geopolitical rise, fragmentation, relative decline	Roots of Habsburg rule in Austria go back to the 13th century and its control of Hungary and other areas through the 16th century, but arguably the peak of its power occurred from the declaration of the Dual Monarchy in 1867 through the beginning of World War I; the war shattered its strength and began the process that led to its dissolution
Ottoman Empire	General geopolitical rise, relative decline over centuries, eventual fragmentation	Undertook various campaigns of expansion from its origins around 1300 that led to a peak of power in the 16th century; by the late 17th century, the empire was already losing major battles and shrinking, and the trajectory of generalized domestic and international decline continued through the late 19th century, when many former territories had been lost, with World War I delivering the death blow
France	General geopolitical rise and relative decline	Achieved two peaks of power as dominant European actor in the eras of Louis XIV and Napoleon; represents persistent role as one among several important post-1815 European powers; industrial dynamism does not match that of the United Kingdom (UK) or United States (or even Germany); persistent but not revitalized power after 1945

Table 2.1—Continued

Case	Rise or Decline Type	Primary Events and Characteristics
Renaissance Italian City-States (Italy)	General geopolitical rise and relative decline	Different city-states reached peak power at different times, but the general trajectory was similar: rising trade and financial influence, partly through maritime power (for Venice, leading to an apex in the 13th and 14th centuries; for Florence, in the 15th century); declines begin in the later 15th century with the rise of more power empires and nation-states, shifting trade patterns, and changing domestic elite politics and economic incentives; represents a largely singular trajectory of gradual rise and decline
China	Rise to major power, relative decline followed by industrialization	Could be counted as a leading economic power before 1800 based on modern GDP estimates, but it was not a consistently influential geopolitical actor outside its own immediate region until the 20th century; moreover, early strength gave way to instability and weakness relative to European powers, as well as invasion and defeat by Japan in the 1930s; began an industrialization drive in the 1970s that has pushed it to the top of world hierarchies in many areas, though this is not so much a case of national renewal as it is of development

SOURCES: Authors' analysis of information from Mazarr, 2022; Kennedy, 1989; other literature on national rise and decline cited earlier in this chapter.

renewal in the face of multiple challenges that threatened the countries' competitive standing.

This review of literatures and historical cases led to an initial, rather stark finding: Very few great powers have managed to generate true national renewal after a significant decline. The most common pattern involves the emergence of multiple factors that undermine a nation's dynamism and competitive standing—the sort of negative spiral documented in the first phase of the study.[1] Once in the grip of such a spiral, great powers seldom shake off the trajectory. Habsburg Spain, the Ottoman and Austro-Hungarian Empires, and the Soviet Union represent examples of powers that declined

---

[1] Mazarr, 2022, pp. 302–303.

from a peak of global influence and never recovered. (We were concerned here with longer-term trends, not short-term retrenchment that led to more immediate changes in their strategic position.[2]) We did not identify a single great power that suffered very significant long-term decline, caused in large measure by domestic socioeconomic stagnation or collapse, and went on to recover its position. Most long-term secular declines have left the ebbing great powers in a fundamentally different absolute and relative position—as with the former Ottoman and Austro-Hungarian Empires, Great Britain, and the Soviet Union.

The first phase of our research strongly emphasized one factor as a source of stagnation and decline: bureaucratic-governmental sclerosis. Such scholars as James Burnham, Mancur Olson, and Walter Scheidel have contended that, over time, nations tend to experience bureaucratic-administrative bloat, governmental stagnation and inefficiency, and rising inequality in ways that threaten the legitimacy of their models.[3] Our analysis concurs that many historical cases of decline do appear to have this aspect in common: The emergence of bureaucratic and political patterns that obstruct growth and innovation also gradually create a popular sense that governing institutions are unresponsive and, in many cases, captured by the wealthy and powerful. When such trends are to blame for national decline, few nations have found a way to reverse their momentum.

There is a more recent category of cases that represents a partial version of national renewal, which consists of nations that have undertaken various economic and, in some cases, broad social reforms in the past half-century to promote stronger growth and innovation. Not all of these are successful cases, but all have involved some degree of policy change to generate national renewal. Possible examples include Britain in the 1970s and 1980s, the United States in the 1980s and 1990s, and Japan from the 2000s to the present. We consider these cases to be *partial* because the

---

[2] For a discussion of such cases of retrenchment, see Paul C. McDonald and Joseph M. Parent, *Twilight of the Titans: Great Power Decline and Retrenchment*, Cornell University Press, 2017.

[3] Francis P. Sempa, "Spengler, Toynbee, Burnham, and the Decline of the West," Russell Kirk Center, January 23, 2022. Mancur Olson and Walter Scheidel's ideas will be discussed at greater length in Chapter 4.

changes undertaken in these years might have made a partial or temporary difference but did not decisively alter the trajectory of the nations as measured by our indicators of national success.

Quantitative Indicators of Decline and Renewal

In addition to reviewing historical cases, we reviewed multiple potential indicators of decline and renewal and evaluated them as possible variables or proxy variables for a quantitative assessment. Any effort to generate quantifiable indexes for national trajectories must confront the challenge of a lack of accurate data for the full period under consideration. Economic historians have sought to assign certain high-level macroeconomic data, such as GDP, as far back as 1600 and well before, but these data are often estimates that might not support detailed year-to-year trend assessments. In some areas, there are no meaningful data available before the 1980s. However, our analysis relies on evidence of the trajectory of national power, not merely top-level comparative assessments, and the available data do not support such a comparison over time. For example, we do not have reliable evidence for national productivity or innovation during the Victorian era or the U.S. Gilded Age that we can use to measure national renewal.

Some analyses have used index or proxy values to assign general trajectories to relative great-power standing in the international system. General studies of great-power hierarchies define fairly simple trajectories as captured by one common measure—the leading powers' standing in global per capita GDP measures, shown in Figure 2.1. These trajectories show a series of hegemons rising to the top of international hierarchies then sustaining relative decline (all so far except the United States), while a few countries (such as Japan) gain relative standing from rapid industrialization. None of these representations depict a pattern of generalized renewal. Both the United States and Great Britain show some degree of recovery after 1973, but this was a product of the Soviet collapse more than true systemic renewal.[4]

---

[4] We researched post-1973 British and U.S. cases to determine whether the Thatcher and Reagan eras reflected true examples of national renewal. These cases have some hallmarks of revitalized national energy and willpower and generated some economic

FIGURE 2.1

Relative Standing of the Great Powers

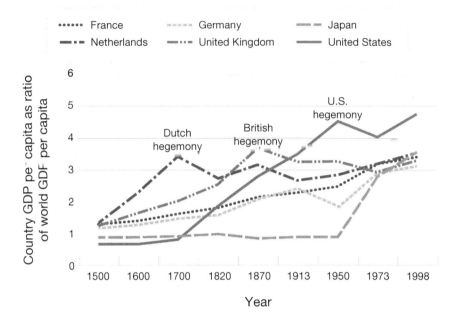

SOURCE: Adapted from Chris Chase-Dunn, Roy Kwon, Kirk Lawrence, and Hiroko Inoue, "Last of the Hegemons," Institute for Research on World-Systems, University of California-Riverside, November 2010.

Other indexes of measurable power from more recent periods (as shown in Figure 2.2) depict a similarly straightforward pattern, reflecting China's general industrialization and growth, persistent U.S. power, India's emergent position, and a continued relative decline of traditional European great powers. Here, too, we see no evidence of broad-based recovery.

In many cases, key economic variables exist within longer-term historical trends that mask or override national conditions or efforts. For example, world per capita GDP skyrocketed in the industrial era after circa 1800. This "hockey stick" advance meant that all industrial countries would experi-

results, but the overall outcomes of these periods did not lay the groundwork for sustained national renewal, especially in the British case.

FIGURE 2.2

Leading States in the International System, 1980–2012, Using Global Power Index

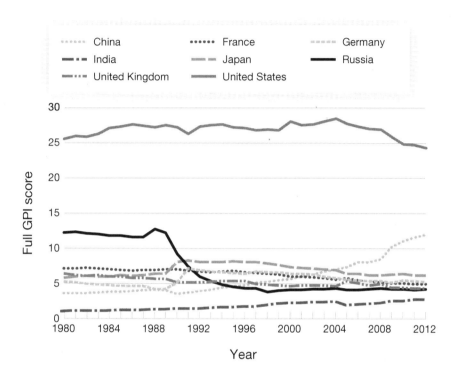

SOURCE: Reproduced from Jacob L. Heim and Benjamin M. Miller, *Measuring Power, Power Cycles, and the Risk of Great-Power War in the 21st Century*, RAND Corporation, RR-2989-RC, 2020, p. 7.

NOTE: GPI = Global Power Index. The GPI includes nuclear weapons, military expenditures, GDP, trade, innovation, governance quality, and population.

ence a dramatic growth in wealth. Differences among industrializing countries were ultimately less significant than distinctions between those that industrialized and those that did not. For example, in the cases of the countries shown in the graph in Figure 2.3, there are no clear rise-and-decline trajectories even though these powers had a complex set of relative position changes from 1500 to 1900. The bigger realities are the broad trends—the growing per capita GDP of all countries after 1800, with several advanc-

FIGURE 2.3

GDP Per Capita, Selected Great Powers, 1500–1900

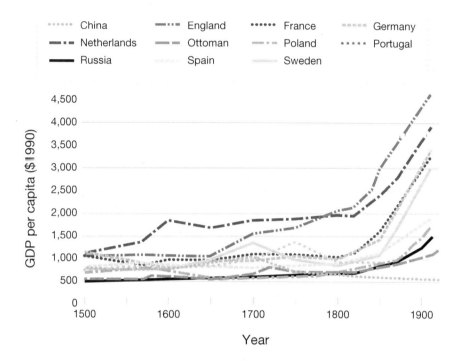

SOURCE: Adapted from Sheilagh Ogilvie, "State Capacity and Economic Growth: Cautionary Tales from History," *National Institute Economic Review*, Vol. 262, No. 1, Autumn 2022, p. 30.

ing more rapidly than the rest—rather than more-nuanced country-specific changes in status.[5]

Figure 2.4 provides a similar perspective in the case of one country. Multiple institutional and technological developments after 1600 contributed to the spiking in British productivity growth before the industrial revolution.

---

[5] One measure of relative regional hegemony that shows similar predictable, unilinear trajectories is discussed in Stephen Watts, Bryan Frederick, Jennifer Kavanagh, Angela O'Mahony, Thomas S. Szayna, Matthew Lane, Alexander Stephenson, and Colin P. Clarke, *A More Peaceful World? Regional Conflict Trends and U.S. Defense Planning*, RAND Corporation, RR-1177-A, 2017, pp. 244–248.

FIGURE 2.4

Permanent Productivity Growth in Britain

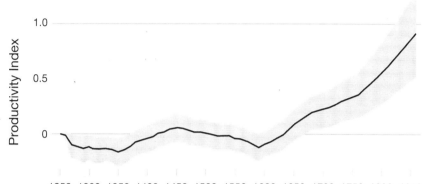

SOURCE: Reproduced from Paul Bouscasse, Emi Nakamura, and Jón Steinsson, "When Did Growth Begin? New Estimates of Productivity Growth in England from 1250 to 1870," National Bureau of Economic Research, Working Paper 28623, revised March 2023, p. 26.

This growth would later level off and stagnate, leading to what some have described as the "British disease" and a perceived crisis of national dynamism that persists to this day.[6] However, this situation represents a relatively straightforward historical juncture rather than a varying trend that could be used to assess rising and falling fortunes. As noted above, this finding suggests that few countries undergo extensive declines and renewals of broad measures of national dynamism; they tend to experience more singular rises and falls.

In sum, qualitative and quantitative indicators tell the same story: Since 1600, international politics has seen no comprehensive cases of national

---

[6] By 2022, Britain badly lagged such countries as the United States, Switzerland, Belgium, Denmark, Luxembourg, and Poland in productivity measures and trailed France and Germany by a notable degree as well (Organisation for Economic Co-operation and Development, "Level of GDP per Capita and Productivity," dataset, undated). See also Nicholas Crafts and Terence C. Mills, "Is the UK Productivity Slowdown Unprecedented?" *National Institute Economic Review*, Vol. 251, February 2020.

renewal after a period of striking relative decline. We turned to a related concept, the idea of anticipatory renewal, as an alternative focus.

CHAPTER 3

A Modified Concept: Anticipatory Renewal

We therefore shifted our focus to identifying great powers that faced the risk of *prospective* decline, began to see their power challenged or their domestic health at risk, and acted to forestall these trends; otherwise put with less intentionality, these powers underwent a natural evolution that helped extricate them from a crisis or semi-decline. We were interested in great powers that confronted failing dynamism and competitive disadvantage through coordinated government action, coalescence of societal actors, or other means to sustain their competitive dynamism. These still constitute cases of national renewal but from less extreme degrees of decay.

To assess anticipatory renewal, we examined factors that produced (1) a general appreciation or, in some cases, formal assessment that some kind of decline or more serious collapse is imminent and (2) an ability or tendency of the society to respond to such signals with productive action. The result is a study of national adaptiveness in the face of prospective or ongoing decline and wherewithal.

We identified three such case studies of most-immediate relevance to our purposes, two of successful renewal and one of a failed effort: Great Britain during the Victorian era (roughly 1830–1900); the United States from the Gilded Age (1870s–1880s) to about World War I (1914–1918), which then had downstream positive results from the 1930s to the 1960s; and the Soviet Union from the 1970s to its dissolution (1989–1990). These three cases met several criteria for selection:

- They involve great powers confronting a variety of internal and external challenges that demanded a response.

- They are all modern cases and thus more likely to have aspects in common with the U.S. case in the 21st century.
- They each involve a great power that had experienced significant dynamism and success in economic growth, industrial output, military power, and global status.
- They each reflect a clear set of events or actions—some more intentional than others—that added up to an agenda of renewal, which either succeeded or failed.

By *renewal*, we mean a process of recovery from imminent stagnation or decline on the part of a major or great power that has previously been at or near top-of-world status in either relative power or in certain absolute measures. Therefore, there are two specific types of national rejuvenation we did not consider. The first is recovery after a major war, as in postwar Germany and Japan, because these postwar renewals responded to different kinds of internal and external challenges to a national model than we have in mind. A second type of renewal that is beyond our focus is rapid economic modernization in societies that might have been large or influential but were not previously considered competitive with world leaders in economic, technological, or military power. Thus, while certainly a form of renewal (and described by its leaders specifically as "national rejuvenation"), China's tremendous advance since the 1970s also falls outside our analytical remit.

Our approach demands some sense of what a successful renewal effort looks like. Because great powers might confront unavoidably growing constraints on their status and influence that vary in severity, their renewal efforts probably cannot be judged by whether they preserve their existing relative power. There is also a question of periodization: A great power's response to impending decline might look either promising or failed for years, even decades, only to eventually bear fruit.[1]

---

[1] Kenneth Pomeranz explains that China illustrates the problem of dividing societies into winners and losers: "For most of history, it would have to be considered an unusually 'successful' society if we use either the criterion of power or that of average material living standards." According to Pomeranz, the modern period that has been classified as a failure is a "blip" in Chinese history. See Kenneth Pomeranz, "Calamities Without Collapse: Environment, Economy, and Society in China, ca. 1800–1949," in Patricia Ann McAnany and Norman Yoffee, eds., *Questioning Collapse: Human Resilience, Eco-*

A further difficulty in identifying and evaluating such cases is that a decline can be impending—and anticipatory renewal required—even when the nation's apparent competitive position remains largely unchanged. Britain's international standing was not measurably decaying from 1820 to about 1870; the competitive price that it was paying for its domestic challenges was not yet obvious. The same could be said about the United States between 1870 and 1920 or even the Soviet Union before about 1985.

Each of these powers could have maintained its overall power at a high level even without reform. There is no way to know what Britain's relative competitive position would have been in 1900 or 1930 had it not undertaken the reform projects of the Victorian era, for example. One could argue that on several broad measures—such as its share of manufacturing output and overall military strength—addressing the accumulating social crises might not have radically affected its standing. If so, then Victorian-era Britain did not renew itself in competitive terms.

Our analysis and research strongly support the idea that national competitiveness is a function of domestic dynamism, willpower, and stability—and therefore that failing to address challenges to those essential qualities, such as those present in early Victorian-era Britain or Gilded Age United States, will eventually eat away at a country's relative strength. Table 3.1 lays out the seven societal characteristics that we have identified as affecting national competitiveness. Emerging challenges and problems in 19th-century Britain and late-19th- and early-20th-century United States held risks of crises in many of these areas. These countries were headed for bigger competitive problems because had they not acted to address these issues. Acting in advance to head off threats to the requirements of competitiveness has provided some nations with sustained advantage, and we therefore conclude that anticipatory renewal is a legitimate phenomenon with real implications for nations' long-term competitive position.

logical Vulnerability, and the Aftermath of Empire, Cambridge University Press, 2010, p. 71.

TABLE 3.1

Causal Links: Anticipated Decline and National Competitive Position

Societal Characteristic	Risks and Challenges Emerging in Britain and the United States, 1820–1920	Potential Impact of Negative Trends on Competitive Position
National will and ambition	In both cases, there was a sense of domestic crisis that could have undermined outward-facing national will.	Ebbing national willpower could reduce support for active foreign policy.
Unified national identity	Challenges, especially those pitting elites against mass publics, could have undermined a sense of common national identity and allegiance	Such a trend would have weakened the nation for future trials; both countries leaned heavily on national solidarity during multiple wars and rivalries.
Shared opportunity	Both countries confronted rising inequality and—absent reform— weak education and public service sectors.	Without reform, these problems would have continually reduced the share of the population able to realize its full potential, as well as weakened the perceived legitimacy of society.
Active state	In both cases, the government was beset with perceptions (and some degree of reality) of corruption and ineffectuality.	This trend could have more seriously injured public faith in public action and undercut efforts to actively seek competitive advantage.
Effective institutions	In both cases, institutions remained broadly effective, but the same trends in perceived corruption and lack of representation threatened to change this condition over time.	Over time, such a trend could have impaired the effectiveness and legitimacy of institutions—as is occurring in the United States at the time of writing.
Learning and adapting mindset	This was not yet under immediate threat in either case, but a continuation of significant social challenges could have produced a reactionary imposition of orthodoxy, which occurred at some moments in both countries.	Such a shift in the mindset of both countries would have imposed significant competitive costs, potentially affecting levels of innovation and adaptation.

Table 3.1—Continued

Societal Characteristic	Risks and Challenges Emerging in Britain and the United States, 1820–1920	Potential Impact of Negative Trends on Competitive Position
Diversity and pluralism	In both cases, economic challenges produced some degree of xenophobic anti-immigrant sentiment, which could have intensified and become more generalized without reform.	Such a trend would have sacrificed some degree of the competitive advantage both countries gained over following decades from being more open and welcoming than autocratic challengers.

SOURCE: This table is based on the research in Mazarr, 2022.

As we looked for cases of anticipatory renewal, we focused on three criteria for assessing successful cases:

- Did the great power develop a set of specific reforms or responses, either through government planning and intent or through the emergent responses of various interests and actors in society that produced measurable results?
- Did the great power remain a great power—coherent, well-governed, competitive in global statecraft, and capable of projecting economic and military power?
- Did the great power's perceived status and influence (including soft power and cultural influence) hold roughly steady?

For our analysis, we selected cases that reflected either a successful or failed example of all or most of these defining characteristics.

CHAPTER 4

Sources of National Decline and Stagnation: A Review of the Literature

Before turning to specific cases of national renewal, we first sought to understand some of the causalities of national renewal and the reasons why nations might ebb in power and dynamism and, in some cases, recover. Therefore, we reviewed the literatures on national rise and decline and on societal collapse and regeneration for clues to such causalities. This chapter presents our findings.

Factors Identified in the First Phase of Research

Any case of national decline is likely to involve a multiplicity of causes—some systemic, some unique to the moment, some based on choice, and some by accident. This causal complexity makes it difficult, if not impossible, to precisely "string together the various episodes, mistakes, and challenges that might have led" to collapse or decline.[1] Nonetheless, a large

---

[1] Miguel A. Centeno, Peter W. Callahan, Paul A. Larcey, and Thayer S. Patterson, "Globalization and Fragility: A Systems Approach to Collapse," in Miguel A. Centeno, Peter W. Callahan, Paul A. Larcey, and Thayer S. Patterson, eds., *How Worlds Collapse: What History, Systems, and Complexity Can Teach About Our Modern World and Fragile Future*, Routledge, 2023, p. 11.

number of studies have surveyed a variety of potential factors as responsible for such processes.[2]

During our historical and theoretical literature review, which generated seven leading characteristics of competitive societies, we uncovered many potential avenues to national decline without the goal of generating a typology for them. The general framework we developed does offer such a typology of decline, if only by implication; Table 3.1 summarizes some of the connections between these seven basic characteristics and national outcomes. The connections are not deterministic, but our research showed that countries that do well across these categories tend to gain competitive advantage. Those connections suggest that decline can be a product of the following:

- *inadequate national ambition or willpower*, expressed in external and internal forms (such as lack of drive for progress, entrepreneurial energy, solidarity-based dynamism)
- *fractured national identity* (such as internal divisions or outright conflict and a lack of sense of common project or mutual responsibility)
- *limited societal opportunity* (such as denying some groups of citizens the opportunity to express their full talents and rising inequality and its effects on legitimacy and solidarity)
- *a weak or ineffectual state role in advancing social dynamism* (such as a lack of adequate public investment, a corrupt or ineffective state system, and bureaucratic ossification)
- *poor-quality institutions* (including military, economic, educational, technological, or other institutions that generate low-quality outputs and are poorly or inadequately staffed, corrupt, or governed by habits of mind that obstruct effectiveness)
- *rigid orthodoxies* (whether political, ideological, religious, or other limits to open-minded learning and adaptation)

---

[2] One recent assessment lists systemic overcomplexity, delaying political authority and cohesion, "corruption, loss of legitimacy or trust, unsustainable inequality, shortsightedness driven by hyperbolic discounting, overuse of resources, misplaced faith in the reliability of advantaged technologies, and an overemphasis on efficiency," as well as "a sclerotic bureaucracy and corrupt elite" (Centeno et al., 2023, p. 12).

- *unitary homogeneity* (such as a lack of significant diversity or pluralism in populations, governing structures, or public sphere ideas).

Classic Challenges to Great Powers: The Literature on National Decline

We also reviewed the work of various scholars and literatures that offer theories of societal decline. Many of these theories are highly qualitative approaches grounded in a subjective assessment of specific cases and sometimes abstract theories of national fate. Some of these approaches have been criticized for simplifying complex historical narratives. We relied on them only as sources of general themes and insights, which then informed but did not guide our research, as in the case studies that follow. Table 4.1 summarizes these theories of decline.

Several broad themes emerge from these theories. First, an emerging *addiction to luxury and decadence* is explored in the work of Ibn Khaldûn, Oswald Spengler, Robert Gilpin, and others, who speak to an ebbing national will and drive for improvement. A second consistent theme, spanning the theories of Immanuel Wallerstein, Joseph Schumpeter, and Gilpin, highlights a *failure to keep pace with the technological or economic demands of an era* as a central feature in national decline. Third, several of these authors (including Paul Kennedy, Joseph Tainter, and Jared Diamond, among others) have also identified *overreach of various kinds*—environmental, resource, geopolitical, or financial—as a third factor of decline.

Fourth, many of these theorists (including Arnold J. Toynbee, Schumpeter, Mancur Olson, and Gilpin) emphasize the ways in which mature industrial societies become *institutionally and bureaucratically constrained and ossified*, with resulting barriers to innovation and change, an increasingly binding intellectual orthodoxy, and a declining degree of legitimacy. Fifth, many of these theorists are concerned with *the role of self-interested or incoherent elite classes* in contributing to national decline—in other words, situations in which state institutions become vehicles for elites to achieve their goals, which leads, in some cases, to the idea of "state capture" by elites or an oligarchy. Variants of this theme emerge in Khaldûn, Toynbee, Olson, Tainter, and others. Sixth, beginning with Khaldûn (but also reflected in

TABLE 4.1

Selected Theories of Societal Decline

Author	Driver of Decline	Related Theories
Ibn Khaldûn (1332–1406)	**Luxury and indolence:** Societies begin with strong group solidarity, community, and common purpose (*asabiyyah*). In a second phase, the energetic nomadic societies become established states and more sedentary in their ways, but strong *asabiyyah* is still present. Such societies reach their peak and then transition to the third phase, in which the now-established leaders and elites become more self-interested, demand luxuries and become indolent, and have a sense of entitlement. Finally, in the fourth phase, such weakened societies become victim to attacks and invasions from rising powers and are destroyed, and the cycle begins again.[a]	Peter Turchin's take on Khaldûn's cyclical approach; other theories about the moral caliber of a society
Edward Gibbon (1737–1794)	**Loss of civic virtue combined with other causes:** Gibbon's argument was meant to apply to Rome and may not necessarily be generalizable, but the core mechanisms certainly apply to many subsequent powers. At the core of his thesis is an argument about the role of civic virtue, individual responsibility, elite honesty, and public spiritedness. The decline of these qualities weakened Rome. Related trends included the role of mercenaries in Roman armies, the effect of the growing Christian religion on what Gibbon saw as traditional Roman values, and political corruption. Rome was further enfeebled by political instability, military overreach and defeats, and the rise of major challengers.[b]	Khaldûn's notions of societal strength; theories of elite commitment to the common good; Kennedy's overstretch theory

Table 4.1—Continued

Author	Driver of Decline	Related Theories
Immanuel Wallerstein (1930–2019)	**Lack of investments in new technologies:** In Wallerstein's World Systems Theory, the core nations gain their position largely by heavily investing in science, technology, and industrial manufacturing, eventually exporting most labor-intensive production to countries in the periphery or semi-periphery. Core nations increase their advantages by controlling the terms of trade and financial flows. Wallerstein himself suggests that core nations have inherent, path-dependent advantages and are likely to decline only slowly, as a product of many other factors noted below (e.g., overreach, internal instability, crisis events, rise of others, excessive use of resources). However, the nature of their advantages also suggests that decline can come about through failure to keep pace with new technologies.[c]	Industrial-era concepts of development
Arnold J. Toynbee (1889–1975)	**Loss of creative power of the creative minority:** Societal dynamism comes from effective and powerful responses to challenges. Those responses are generated by the creative minority in a society, which generates answers to both external and material challenges, as well as internal challenges dealing with social unity. However, over time, the creative minority transforms into a dominant minority more devoted to preserving established institutions and ways of doing business than to creativity or innovation. It becomes more coercive, imposing its perspectives on society, which generate orthodoxies that stifle innovation. This leads to a loss of legitimacy for the dominant majority. The society becomes less able to respond to new challenges and tends to decline.[d]	Other theories that stress the role of self-interested elites; Khaldûn's notions of luxury and self-serving indolence

Table 4.1—Continued

Author	Driver of Decline	Related Theories
Oswald Spengler (1880–1936)	**Moral decline and decadence:** Spengler's cyclical theory is similar in some ways to Khaldûn's in that it stresses an energetic period of foundation and growth followed by a period of moral decline, self-interest, and a collapse of solidarity. The result is a decadent society devoted to the pursuit of luxury and pleasure: The dynamic energy and drive to compete is lost, social attitudes become more cynical and hardened, creativity dims, and the society declines.[e]	Khaldûn's theory of luxury-based decline; more-recent culturalist analysis of national fates, including Samuel Huntington's later work and the work of Lawrence Harrison[f]
Joseph Schumpeter (1883–1950)	**Failure to adapt to new ideas or new technological developments:** Mature capitalist states will tend to generate elements of stagnation and ossification that constrain their dynamism and potentially lead to decline. These elements include the rise of constraining bureaucratic structures, the growth of satisfied elements of the population less interested in fomenting creative destruction, and a gradual ebbing of the entrepreneurial spirit. A central theme is the loss of creative energy of such societies.[g]	Emphasis on the power of knowledge in economic development and industrialization by Mokyr and others[h]
Paul Kennedy (1945–)	**Military overstretch:** Great powers that achieve their position through economic dynamism, technological leadership, and the resulting fiscal and military power tend to acquire multiple international commitments and tend toward overreach—a situation in which the costs of their commitments outstrip the financial and military capacity of the nation. However, the most dynamic and technologically advanced great powers can partially mitigate this outcome through the productive and growth-generating innovations they generate.[i]	Broader literature on overstretch, including more-recent analyses of great-power rivalries; discussions of the role of stable finances and the effects of "state fiscal distress": "The state becomes effectively starved of the revenue and authority needed to combat violent outbursts, or to resolve the underlying tension through spending programs aimed at reducing popular immiseration, often losing legitimacy in the process."[j]

Table 4.1—Continued

Author	Driver of Decline	Related Theories
Robert Gilpin (1930–2018)	**Diminishing returns:** As the size and the extent of its control increase, a state starts to experience decreasing returns to scale at some point in time. The protection costs increase while production and consumption increase. Nations experience many classic forms of overreach and exhaustion: slowing economic growth and productivity, rising costs of sustaining the international system (including war), corruption associated with affluence and entitlement, and the political costs of generating more resources. The downward spiral of rising consumption and declining investments results in economic, military, and political decline.[j]	Closely related to many theories of national or imperial overreach and thresholds of sustainable power, from Khaldûn to Kennedy
Mancur Olson (1932–1998)	**Social rigidities from logic of narrow interest group self-interest:** Over time, mature societies see the accumulation of narrow interest groups (or "distributional coalitions"), which reflect their own self-interest. By opposing policies that threaten their self-interest and because of their large number and accumulating power, these groups generate a degree of societal rigidity and lack of flexibility, which causes national stagnation and decline in part by limiting economic growth.[k]	Jonathan Rauch's concept of "demosclerosis," which builds on Olson's work;[l] ideas about bureaucratic-administrative overreach and rigidities and the role of self-interested elites[m]
Joseph Tainter (1949–)	**Social complexity leading to resource exhaustion:** As societies "continue to expand and encounter new and bigger challenges," demanding more and more division of labor, specialty bureaucratic and technical functions, and need to control larger areas, they become more and more complex and outrun the resources available to support such complexity. This leads to collapse, with the Roman and Maya empires being offered as key cases. Ultimately, such societies run into a challenge that fractures their now-brittle structure.[n]	Theories of Olson, Gilpin, Goldstone, and Scheidel

Table 4.1—Continued

Author	Driver of Decline	Related Theories
Jack Goldstone (1953–)	**Excess elites:** A demographic structural theory of elite overproduction in which an oversupply of elites lead to intra-elite competition and social decay.[o]	Many classic and recent treatments of the role of elites (though few stress the overproduction issue); related to classic Malthusian theories of population overproduction
Walter Scheidel (1966–)	**Self-interested and warring elites:** Multiple scholars have argued that hierarchies tend to emerge and solidify in societies, "feeding inequality and corruption, pitting elites against one another, and constructing sclerotic institutions that struggle to address impending problems when they conflict with vested elite interests"; Scheidel argues that the degenerative pattern of elite capture is only broken by major instabilities—truly major war, revolution, or plagues—that shake the society to its foundations.[p]	Tainter and Goldstone's more general theories of the elite capture of social institutions
Jared Diamond (1937–)	**Unsustainable environmental practices:** Multiple forms of environmental degradation undercut the resource base of societies, cause civil strife, and generate other fatal problems.[q] Some theories focus on climate change as a source, though in previous eras this was an exogenous factor rather than the result of social practice.[r]	Classic Malthusian theories of resource exhaustion; the collapse literature's emphasis on environmental crises or long-term pressure, sometimes spurred by unsustainable actions; some recent literature questions Diamond's nomination of this factor as determinative in key cases

Table 4.1—Continued

Author	Driver of Decline	Related Theories

[a] Ibn Khaldûn, *The Muqaddimah: An Introduction to History – Abridged Edition*, ed. by N. J. Dawood, trans. by Franz Rosenthal, Princeton University Press, 2005; Syed Farid Alatas, "Luxury, State and Society: The Theme of Enslavement in Ibn Khaldun," *Journal of Historical Sociology*, Vol. 30, No. 1, March 2017; Muhsin Mahdi, *Ibn Khaldûn's Philosophy of History: A Study in the Philosophic Foundation of the Science of Culture*, University of Chicago Press, 1964.

[b] Edward Gibbon, *The History of the Decline and Fall of the Roman Empire*, Strahan & Cadell, originally published 1776–1789.

[c] Immanuel Wallerstein, *World-Systems Analysis: An Introduction*, Duke University Press, 2004; Immanuel Wallerstein, "The Rise and Future Demise of the World Capitalist System: Concepts for Comparative Analysis," *Comparative Studies in Society and History*, Vol. 16, No. 4, September 1974.

[d] Arnold Toynbee, *A Study of History*, Oxford University Press, 1934–1961.

[e] Oswald Spengler, *The Decline of the West*, George Allen & Unwin, 1926.

[f] Lawrence E. Harrison and Samuel P. Huntington, eds., *Culture Matters: How Values Shape Human Progress*, Basic Books, 2000. Another example is the simple "individualist versus communitarian" dichotomy proposed by some analysts in the 1980s who were anxious to account for East Asian economic progress. For example, see George C. Lodge and Ezra F. Vogel, eds., *Ideology and National Competitiveness: An Analysis of Nine Countries*, Harvard Business School Press, 1987.

[g] Thomas K. McCraw, *Prophet of Innovation: Joseph Schumpeter and Creative Destruction*, Harvard University Press, 2007.

[h] See Joel Mokyr, *A Culture of Growth: The Origins of the Modern Economy*, Princeton University Press, 2016; and Joel Mokyr, "The Intellectual Origins of Modern Economic Growth," *Journal of Economic History*, Vol. 65, No. 2, June 2005.

[i] Kennedy, 1989.

[i] Daniel Hoyer, James S. Bennett, Harvey Whitehouse, Pieter François, Kevin Feeney, Jill Levine, Jenny Reddish, Donagh Davis, and Peter Turchin, "Flattening the Curve: Learning the Lessons of World History to Mitigate Societal Crises," SocArXiv, last updated July 19, 2022, p. 4.

[j] Robert Gilpin, *War and Change in International Politics*, Cambridge University Press, 1981.

[k] Mancur Olson, *The Rise and Decline of Nations: Economic Growth, Stagflation, and Social Rigidities*, Yale University Press, 1982.

[l] Jonathan Rauch, *Demosclerosis*, Random House, 1994.

[m] Luke Kemp, "Diminishing Returns on Extraction," in Miguel A. Centeno, Peter W. Callahan, Paul A. Larcey, and Thayer S. Patterson, eds., *How Worlds Collapse: What History, Systems, and Complexity Can Teach About Our Modern World and Fragile Future*, Routledge, 2023, pp. 38, 44, 50–52.

[n] Daniel Hoyer, "Decline and Fall, Growth and Spread, or Resilience? Approaches to Studying How and Why Societies Change," pre-print of essay forthcoming in *Journal of World History*, SocArXiv, January 7, 2022, p. 2. See also Rebecca Storey and Glenn R. Storey, "Requestioning the Classic Maya Collapse and the Fall of the Roman Empire: Slow Collapse," in Robert K. Faulseit, ed., *Beyond Collapse: Archaeological Perspectives on Resilience, Revitalization, and Transformation in Complex Societies*, Center for Archaeological Investigations, Occasional Paper No. 42, 2016.

[o] Jack A. Goldstone, *Revolution and Rebellion in the Early Modern World*, University of California Press, 1991.

[p] Kemp, 2023, p. 47.

[q] Jared Diamond, *Collapse: How Societies Choose to Succeed or Fail*, Viking Penguin, 2005. See also Niall Ferguson, *Doom: The Politics of Catastrophe*, Penguin, 2021.

[r] Harvey Weiss, ed., *Megadrought and Collapse: From Early Agriculture to Angkor*, Oxford University Press, 2017.

Spengler, Tainter, Olson, and others) many theorists stress the role of *declining solidarity and socio-national commitment* among the elites and broader population as contributing to decline.

These themes—especially those of rising decadence, bureaucratic-administrative fetters, and self-interested elites—paint a grim but coherent picture of aging, complex societies: They are infused with conceptions of entitlement and a growing affinity for wealth and luxury, constrained by increasingly dense bureaucratic-administrative structures, run by groups of self-interested elites who advocate for their own benefits and end up undermining the legitimacy of public and private institutions alike, and are increasingly fractured by internal disputes. Taken together, these components of entitlement and decadence, social complexity and bureaucratic shackles, a lack of elite commitment to long-term renewal and the common good, and a loss of solidarity create a consistent vision of national decline across our case studies. This combination of factors produces a general trend toward an accumulating loss of energy, drive, and adaptive capacity, which is discussed with remarkable consistency by all these theorists.

Steven Ward has made a related argument: National decline is not merely the result of domestic social fragmentation and instability—it can also help produce such a result. As great powers decline, the process generally exacerbates domestic psychological and political conflicts in ways that intensify sociopolitical conflict. Decline, he argues, can "drive substate groups apart and incentivize hostility between them."[3] This finding emphasizes the powerful dynamic that can emerge between decline and domestic dysfunction.

In a negative sense, many of these theories share a view that, once established, the habits, norms, and interests of such a trajectory become very difficult to break. Olson, Scheidel, and Toynbee all speak to the potential need for massive social dislocation to break out of the grip of accumulated elite interests. Olson and others have argued that postwar German and Japanese progress, or even the postwar U.S. boom achieved in relatively equitable terms, came from a substantial shaking up of the elite groups—either essentially wiping out a significant number of them or forcibly opening many new avenues for social progress.

---

[3] Steven Ward, "Decline and Disintegration: National Status Loss and Domestic Conflict in Post-Disaster Spain," *International Security*, Vol. 46, No. 4, Spring 2022, p. 128.

More-Extreme Examples: The Literature on Societal Collapse

We reviewed an additional literature on societal collapse and regeneration for clues as to the possible sources of national stagnation and decline. While this literature deals with a more-extreme form of national decline than the kind that we have in mind in this report, which involves a more gradual ebbing of dynamism, it might perhaps provide clues about similar drivers of more gradual national rise and decline.

Literature on societal collapse has tried to identify variables that trigger a societal breaking point that leads to *collapse*, which is typically defined as a dramatic loss of social cohesion and complexity. An opposing counter-collapse literature has emerged, which argues that many alleged stories of collapse are based on weak evidence and ultimately reflect stories of persistence and regeneration.[4] This literature cites a variety of causes for collapse but emphasizes several notable factors—which in many cases overlap with the seven social characteristics affecting national competitiveness—that can help us understand the sources of decline and renewal.[5]

The first such issue is *the importance of institutions*. This emerged as one of our seven qualities of competitively successful nations, and it also features prominently in assessments of national collapse and resilience.[6] A consistent theme is the role of good institutions and the rise and corrupt or ineffectual ones in the period of decline, which, for example, was true of the Spanish and Ottoman Empires. The literature on collapses also stresses the role of weakening institutions that cannot recover their effectiveness or legitimacy in the process of societal collapse.

---

[4] Hoyer, 2022.

[5] For causes of collapse, see Joseph A. Tainter, "How Scholars Explain Collapse," in Miguel A. Centeno, Peter W. Callahan, Paul A. Larcey, and Thayer S. Patterson, eds., *How Worlds Collapse: What History, Systems, and Complexity Can Teach About Our Modern World and Fragile Future*, Routledge, 2023, pp. 25–36. Tainter cites such factors as climate change, invasions, rebellions, environmental degradation, catastrophes, and sudden changes in trade patterns.

[6] See the sources cited in Hoyer, 2022, p. 8.

A second theme in the literature on collapse and regeneration is *resilience*, broadly defined as the ability of a society or institution to sustain its functioning in the face of changing environments.[7] Resilient societies are able to bounce back from major challenges because of a set of qualities that has been identified in multiple analyses.[8] Resilience is typically a function of a combination of socio-psychological issues in a population (the ability to withstand crises or disasters and retain social coherence and willpower) and institutional factors (the existence of effective institutions capable of dealing with stressful events). Collapse has occurred in societies in which these characteristics ebbed or were never significantly present to begin with. Some degree of societal resilience would seem to be essential for processes of renewal.

The literature on collapse nominates a third theme relevant to our topic of national renewal: the importance of *tipping points*. This is more a question for collapse than gradual decline, but it can be difficult to identify when a system will enter a steeper decline or collapse. Tipping points can arrive with a combination of events that work together to create a synergistic and decisive effect that could not have been predicted in advance, sometimes called "synchronous failures."[9] Successful examples of national renewal involve, at least in part, anticipating and avoiding tipping points that could lead to more serious national decline.

Finally, the collapse literature emphasizes the importance of feedback loops in driving processes of collapse. Single factors are never responsible for outcomes as broad and comprehensive as societal collapse: Typically, a set of such factors emerges that becomes subject to *feedback loops* in which each factor begins to exacerbate the others. For example, failing political institutions can make it impossible to solve major social problems, which

---

[7] Ronald K. Faulseit, *Beyond Collapse: Archaeological Perspectives on Resilience, Revitalization, and Transformation in Complex Societies*, Southern Illinois University Press, 2016; Glenn M. Schwartz and John J. Nichols, *After Collapse: The Regeneration of Complex Societies*, University of Arizona Press, 2010.

[8] Nassim Nicholas Taleb, *Antifragile: Things That Gain from Disorder*, Random House, 2012; National Research Council, *Disaster Resilience: A National Imperative*, National Academies Press, 2012.

[9] Centeno et al., 2023, pp. 13, 15.

then undermine legitimacy and spark polarization, which further damages the strength of political institutions. In a positive sense, systemic dynamics of well-functioning societies create feedback loops that reinforce energy, dynamism, and social cohesion.[10] The first part of our research stressed the same basic theme by noting that such feedback loops, whether helpful or destructive, could emerge among the seven characteristics of competitive societies.

Summary: Factors Associated with National Decline

Looking across these three literatures, we identified six broad factors that these theories have traditionally associated with national decline:

1. *weakness in national spirit, ambition, or willpower,* sometimes connected to a sense of entitlement and an affection for luxury
2. *institutional and bureaucratic ossification and decay,* leading to either ineffectiveness of institutions or corruption, or both
3. *self-interested or fractured elite classes and a perception of social divisions and lack of shared opportunity*
4. *failure to keep pace with the economic and technological demands of an era,* specifically in the sense of an inability to align to an age's competitive paradigm
5. *weakening sense of national unity and solidarity* as political fragmentation and social conflict grow
6. *outstripping the resource base of the society* in terms of finances, energy, or environment.

Taken together, these factors add up to two larger dynamics. One is the general resilience of a society—the combination of positive or negative aspects of the above dynamics in ways that makes a society brittle or robust in the face of challenges. The second is the presence of damaging feedback loops among multiple variables, especially among bureaucratic ossifica-

---

[10] Centeno et al., 2023, pp. 13–14.

tion, exogenous events that threaten societies, and the role of self-interested elites. These feedback loops can create a momentum toward decline that becomes very difficult to arrest.

These dynamics then gave us one additional lens for assessing the case studies and the broader question of national renewal. Through examining processes of renewal, we were able to devise strategies to arrive at the positive side of these factors.

CHAPTER 5

Case Studies of National Renewal: Essential Narratives

In the appendixes, we offer detailed analysis of the following three primary case studies: Victorian-era Britain, post–Gilded Age United States, and late–Cold War Soviet Union. In this chapter, we briefly summarize the basic facts of each of the cases, including their lessons for thinking about the issue of renewal.

The cases focus on internal developments within the three countries as sources of national renewal. Partly, this focus is a product of the way in which we define *renewal*—nations that find a way to reverse a trajectory of decline through the effects of inherent characteristics or intentional policy, which aim at improving the domestic engine of dynamism. In theory, those intentional policies could be aimed abroad (for example, the seizing of territory or resources), but our research clearly suggests that such adventurism does not provide a sustainable route to national competitiveness. During certain eras, a country's external sources of wealth—such as colonies—can underwrite domestic reforms and initiatives. However, our research implies that such advantages are not typically the sources of national renewal themselves. When nations confront specific challenges (such as resource shortages), expansionist strategies (such as seizure of colonies) are not as sustainable as other approaches (such as innovation), reforms to improve the effectiveness of institutions, new diplomatic agreements, and regulatory changes to promote greater production.

It could be argued that both successful cases we explore in this chapter represent the same essential phenomenon: increasing state action on behalf of what could be characterized as progressive social change. To be clear, this choice of cases and our analysis do not imply any judgment about broader political issues. Some of the social problems identified in both cases, such as incomplete voting rights and child labor, were shared agendas across elements of the political spectrum at the time. On other issues, such as environmental and labor conditions, the social challenges were clear and undeniable. Both Great Britain and the United States could perhaps have chosen other means to address them; the argument here is not that state action of a particular type was the defining route to success but that a grassroots social movement to address challenges was key.

We also conducted extensive research into two other possible cases of renewal—Great Britain and the United States in the 1970s and 1980s. In both cases, governments came to power determined to revive the perception and reality of national dynamism. They pursued bold agendas of reform, largely built around deregulation, tax cuts, and efforts to boost private-sector innovation and investment. In both cases, they chalked up important achievements, particularly in the U.S. case, to restore some sense of national optimism and mission.[1]

However, we did not find that these undeniable bursts of reform achieved anything like broad-based national renewal in either case. This is not a function of the political character of those reforms being more neoliberal and free-market oriented than state-led reform and solutions. Indeed, the wider project identifies many ways in which flourishing markets and grassroots (rather than centrally directed) solutions are essential to national competitiveness and parallel ways in which ossifying centralized bureaucracy can choke off national dynamism. Our judgment about these cases was strictly a product of the empirical results of the 1970s and 1980s economic and social changes in Britain and the United States: In neither case did they establish

---

[1] Some of the sources reviewed for the British case include Patrick Minford, "Evaluating Mrs. Thatcher's Reforms: Britain's 1980s Economic Reform Program," in Francesco Giavazzi, Francesco Lefebvre D'Ovidio, and Alberto Mingardi, eds., *The Liberal Heart of Europe*, Palgrave Macmillan, 2021; Lucio Baccaro and Chris Howell, *Trajectories of Neoliberal Transformation: European Industrial Relations Since the 1970s*, Cambridge University Press, 2017; James Thomas, "'Bound In by History': The Winter of Discontent in British Politics, 1979–2004," *Media, Culture & Society*, Vol. 29, No. 2, 2007; Earl A. Reitan, *The Thatcher Revolution: Margaret Thatcher, John Major, Tony Blair, and the Transformation of Modern Britain, 1979–2001*, Rowman & Littlefield Publishers, 2003; and Andrew Gamble, *Britain in Decline: Economic Policy, Political Strategy and the British State*, St. Martin's Press, 1994.

a sustainable new model that produced decades of competitive advantage.[2] Some subsequent positive economic changes (such as the U.S. information technology boom of the 1990s) emerged for reasons that were, at best, indirectly related to the reform agendas. In other cases, such as social solidarity and political stability, the agendas of those years did not lay the foundation for long-term national strength. This is, again, not a referendum on the ideological cast of those reforms, but a judgment of their outcomes. Therefore, we did not include them as cases of national renewal.

Victorian-Era Britain

By the early 19th century, Britain was already a leading great power: It was, by many measures, the world's chief maritime power, it was already an economic and financial powerhouse, and it was poised to benefit disproportionately from the first industrial revolution. But by the mid-1800s, Britain was also confronted by a series of daunting social, political, and economic challenges: the human and environmental toll of industrialization, perceived corruption and ineffectiveness of political institutions, control of politics by a small group of landowning elites, rising economic inequality, and more. There is no way to be certain how much competitive effect these challenges would have had on Britain, but as we note, our first-phase analysis strongly suggests that they could have weakened the country's coherence, finances, political stability, and economic performance in serious ways if left unaddressed.

Between the 1820s and the 1880s, a wave of reform swept over multiple areas of British life. Major legislation expanded the voting franchise,

---

[2] On the British case, see John Van Reenen, "The Economic Legacy of Mrs. Thatcher Is a Mixed Bag," London School of Economics, April 10, 2013; Miriam E. David, "What Were the Lasting Effects of Thatcher's Legacy for Families In the UK?" in Stephen Farrall and Colin Hay, eds., *The Legacy of Thatcherism: Assessing and Exploring Thatcherite Social and Economic Policies*, British Academy Original Paperbacks, 2014; Raphaële Espiet-Kilty, "The Legacy of Thatcherism in Question: An Introduction," *Observatoire de la société britannique*, Vol. 17, 2015; and Kevin Albertson and Paul Stepney, "1979 and All That: A 40-Year Reassessment of Margaret Thatcher's Legacy on Her Own Terms," *Cambridge Journal of Economics*, Vol. 44, No. 2, March 2020.

addressed working conditions for women and children, expanded educational opportunities, addressed the environmental cost of industrialization, and much more. Importantly, this agenda was not planned out by the British government or a single set of reformers: It reflected a complex, shifting, grassroots recognition of multiple challenges by different groups in society. The result was a mixed and halting but ultimately comprehensive set of reforms that, as Table 5.1 suggests, addressed many of the sources of potential national decline.

Of particular interest in the British case was the role of elites, including selected members of the landed aristocracy, in supporting elements of these reforms. This support was often based on self-interest; in particular, as the franchise expanded, elites knew that political success depended in part on attracting support from the middle and eventually working classes. (It is also worth pointing out that this system depended on refusing to expand any such franchise to Britain's colonial possessions while continuing to benefit from them well into the 20th century. The public-spiritedness of elites extended almost exclusively to the domestic realm.) But some reformers were largely altruistic, and, ultimately, a critical dynamic was the capacity of a great power's elite to recognize problems and implement reforms.

Britain's response demonstrated national resilience in the face of multiple threats and challenges—the ability of the political and social system to identify problems, develop practical solutions, and carry them out—that kept British power grounded in a strong and dynamic foundation for decades. Through these reforms, Britain created a feedback loop across multiple factors—elite commitment to the common good, expanded political and educational opportunities, improved public welfare—that generated dynamic energy.

Post–Gilded Age United States

A second case study deals with the period just after that of the British case—the United States from the late 19th to the early 20th centuries (with echoes into the 1960s). Like Britain in the early 19th century, the post–Gilded Age United States confronted a set of significant and potentially growing social

TABLE 5.1

Addressing Sources of National Decline: Britain in the Victorian Era

Source of Decline	Element in Renewal?	Case Evidence
Weakness in national spirit, ambition, or willpower	Yes	Reforms were justified in part by reference to nationalism and solidarity and, in some cases, a sense of common project; collectively, these reforms bolstered national energy.
Institutional and bureaucratic ossification and decay	Yes	There was a perception (somewhat exaggerated) of a corrupt political system giving way to political reforms and institutional responses that revalidated institutions; bureaucracy was not an issue.
Self-interested or fractured elite classes and a perception of social divisions and lack of shared opportunity	Yes	One of the most important aspects of the reform drive was the role of elites in working for the common good; many reforms had the practical effect of expanding opportunity.
Failure to keep pace with the economic and technological demands of the era	Only prospective	Britain was emerging as a powerhouse of the first industrial revolution; reforms were essential to maintain Britain's competitive position in general, but in and of themselves, they did not align Britain to the demands of the era.
Weakening sense of national unity and solidarity	Yes	The reforms were grounded in a sense of common purpose, more strongly tied the elites to the common people, and reaffirmed the legitimacy of the national project.
Outstripping the resource base of the society	Only prospective	Social and political challenges would have eventually led to an unsustainable drain on finances and other resources (but this was not yet in evidence).

and political challenges that threatened to undermine the country's advance to global predominance.

As in the British case, we cannot know for certain what impact these challenges would have had if left unaddressed. The United States was a burgeoning industrial power likely to continue expanding its relative economic and technological power even without the surge of reform and resulting renewal that took place in this era. Many economic indicators (such as industrialization per capita, real wage growth, expansion of railroads, overall economic growth) were showing astonishing gains. However, as in the British case, these challenges would have caused instability, hurt national solidarity, probably cut back economic growth, and had other effects that mitigated U.S. power had the United States not taken action.

The period from roughly 1870 to 1900 is known as the United States' Gilded Age. Alongside striking economic progress came rising inequality, social tensions over workers' rights, the environmental and social risks of uncontrolled industrialization, and elements of political corruption, including close connections between business interests and political actors. In response, a loosely affiliated set of politicians, activists, and wealthy reformers who believed that the challenges of the Gilded Age had put future stability and solidarity of U.S. society in danger led what became known as the *Progressive movement.*

As Table 5.2 suggests, this renewal was very much about shared opportunity, social equality, and a renewed commitment, partly between a group of public-spirited elites and the general public. It was thus a narrower version of renewal than that seen in the British case. It helped to create a constructive feedback loop among new public programs and elites (including business leaders) who supported selected reforms, as well as a sense of politicians being on the people's side. It demonstrated a degree of resilience on the part of U.S. society, at least in the face of threatening socioeconomic trends.

Late–Cold War Soviet Union

The third case represents an example of failed national renewal. By the late 1970s, the Soviet Union faced fundamental dilemmas that began with the role of the Communist party, which could neither be escaped nor reformed. It had a stultifying bureaucracy, state-run industries falling into disrepair and lagging ever further behind leading industrial nations, an overburdened state budget (partly because of dozens of foreign commitments in service to Marxist-Leninist ideology), and corruption and rent-seeking throughout the system.

TABLE 5.2

Addressing Sources of National Decline: Post–Gilded Age United States

Source of Decline	Element in Renewal?	Case Evidence
Weakness in national spirit, ambition, or willpower	Yes	National energy and willpower remained significant but were partly undermined by social and political instability and growing doubts about the system's sustainability.
Institutional and bureaucratic ossification and decay	Only prospective	The U.S. political system continued to function, and bureaucratic obstacles were not yet the key barriers to renewal; social challenges would eventually have affected the U.S. political system but had not yet begun to do so.
Self-interested or fractured elite classes and a perception of social divisions and lack of shared opportunity	Yes	As in Britain, many U.S. elites were involved in various elements of the reforms; those reforms increased shared opportunity.
Failure to keep pace with the economic and technological demands of the era	Only prospective	The United States was becoming an industrial titan, addressing challenges that otherwise would likely have impaired this progress.
Weakening sense of national unity and solidarity	Yes	Beginning in the 1880s, social, economic, and political reforms were justified in part by appeals to national pride and solidarity.
Outstripping the resource base of the society	Only prospective	The challenges had not yet begun to undermine the nation's financial or resource base for success.

The case describes the efforts of Mikhail Gorbachev and other reformers to generate the sort of anticipatory national renewal that was achieved in the other cases and the reasons for their failure. As Table 5.3 notes, those reasons were many: The Soviet Union suffered from every major source of national decline cataloged above.

The Soviet case illustrates the immense risk that can emerge with a society afflicted by nearly all sources of decline. Together, they created a deadly feedback loop in which ebbing solidarity and willpower, bureaucratic bar-

TABLE 5.3

Addressing Sources of National Decline: Late–Cold War Soviet Union

Source of Decline	Element in Failed Renewal?	Case Evidence
Weakness in national spirit, ambition, or willpower	Yes	National energy flagged because of a sense of stagnation and bureaucratic roadblocks.
Institutional and bureaucratic ossification and decay	Yes	Soviet bureaucracy was infamously gridlocked, which constrained any sense of reform, and the Communist party was an institutional roadblock to change.
Self interested or fractured elite classes and a perception of social divisions and lack of shared opportunity	Yes	Elites in many instances avoided or undermined reforms that would have threatened their position.
Failure to keep pace with the economic and technological demands of the era	Yes	The primary upshot of the multiple challenges was to slow the USSR's ability to keep up with the late-industrial or information age.
Weakening sense of national unity and solidarity	Yes	A sense of commitment to the national project was weakened even within the USSR; solidarity among parts of the Soviet Union and the Warsaw Pact was collapsing.
Outstripping the resource base of the society	Yes	Financially and in energy terms, the Soviet system had become unsustainable, and reforms worsened the situation.

riers to change, self-interested elites, and slowing technological and innovative potential all exacerbated one another. These sources of decline were then crowned with the ultimate roadblock to renewal—the Communist party itself—which imposed rigid orthodoxies and established conformism and ideological purity as the basis for advancement. As a result, whereas the Russian people and, to a degree, the Soviet government had shown tremendous resilience during the Second World War, by the 1980s, the Soviet system no longer displayed such characteristics. It had become a brittle, vulnerable shell. It is possible that more sensible and gradual reforms could have kept the system plugging along, but there could be no full-scope renewal.

CHAPTER 6

Characteristics Associated with National Renewal

We derived several primary characteristics associated with national renewal from our surveys of the general literature and our research into the British, U.S., and Soviet cases. One difficulty was distinguishing factors associated specifically with the challenge of national renewal from the larger and more general list of qualities that contribute to national strength and dynamism. Although that distinction is neither simple nor clear-cut, some of the factors discussed in this chapter are common to our first-phase assessment of the societal characteristics that produce competitive advantage more generally; however, they also appear in cases of renewal and rise and are particularly relevant to those challenges.

It is important to note that the requirements listed below are not independent—these criteria must all be met for a relatively comprehensive form of renewal to emerge. Yet it could be argued that achieving such an effort (that is, meeting all these criteria for change) is very rare and that only a severe crisis or even war or collapse would impose a sufficient shock on a nation to prompt serious attention to all these steps. Walter Scheidel makes a similar argument about inequality, suggesting that it tends to increase as a general secular trend—as elites find ways to hoard more resources of societies—unless and until a truly dramatic event, such as a major war or revolution, intervenes.[1]

Our case studies suggest that versions of anticipatory renewal can be prompted by a rising sense of urgency in a society without an actual war or

---

[1] Walter Scheidel, *The Great Leveler: Violence and the History of Inequality from the Stone Age to the Twenty-First Century*, Princeton University Press, 2018.

revolution. An accumulation of enough troubling economic, political, and social events and trends can prompt various actors in the country to see a need to take action. However, the relative lack of true cases of large-scale renewal in the modern era may speak to the difficulty of achieving all the demands of national renewal absent a catastrophe.

A Clear Recognition of Key Problems

The first step toward any form of national or organizational renewal is always a serious recognition of a problem or set of problems and an awareness that change is required. In the case of issues of national decline (or stagnation) and renewal, this takes the form of populations and elites recognizing that their country runs the risk of falling behind and losing its desired status in world politics or becoming vulnerable to a specific rival.[2] Diagnosis can be supported by informal or formalized processes to assess the nation's relative position and social condition. In nearly all cases, the task of renewal is complicated by the fact that a nation in decline has many problems to solve and that multiple challenges must be recognized. Sometimes a single leadership group can apprehend many challenges (as in the Soviet case), but, often, the recognition of distinct challenges emerges among different groups in the society. Together, these perceptions contribute to a general awareness that reform is necessary.[3]

Whether it galvanizes an opposition movement to push for alternative policies or opens a policy window for implementing reforms,[4] such a recognition is necessary to address cases in which simple solutions to general declines are inadequate. Without political will or alignment stemming from

---

[2] In discussing an important criterion for renewal in the British case, Aaron Friedberg refers to the necessity of "internal consensus on the existence, nature, and extent of unfavourable changes, not just in one area but in several simultaneously." See Aaron L. Friedberg, *The Weary Titan: Britain and the Experience of Relative Decline, 1895–1905*, Princeton University Press, 2010, p. 290.

[3] Hay, 1999.

[4] For opposition movements, see Robert Ralston, "Make Us Great Again: The Causes of Declinism in Major Powers," *Security Studies*, Vol. 31, No. 4, 2022. For policy windows for implementing reforms, see Hay, 1999.

a broad-based recognition of the problem, it is likely that subsequent efforts will fail.

This conclusion is supported by evidence from several components of our research. In both the British and U.S. case studies, various groups in society recognized the risks inherent to several ongoing social, economic, and political trends and believed that the nation needed to respond or face decline. In contrast, in examples of long-term decline, such as those of the Ottoman Empire and the Soviet Union, there was an inability to diagnose the core problem—or even admit that there was one—until it was too late to make a meaningful difference. The importance of self-awareness comes up as at least an implicit theme in many of the theories of decline catalogued in Chapter 5, and the first phase of our research stressed the importance of a learning mentality, which begins with an ongoing drive to assess a nation's current condition.

Such national self-reflection can be triggered by an external event. In the case of Meiji Japan, the visit of Commodore Matthew Perry with his large warships in 1853 impressed on Japan that wholesale reform was required to withstand the challenge posed by the West. Loss in a major war commonly spurs self-critique, exemplified by the sense of malaise and crisis in the United States after the Vietnam War or the aftermath of the Soviet invasion of Afghanistan.

Achieving such a clear diagnosis of the situation demands a general openness to new ideas that may disrupt the status quo and an ability to engage in reflection and self-criticism, including a willingness to tolerate criticisms of existing practices and the identification of problematic trends. Rigorous self-assessments must also be based on accurate and relevant information drawn from reliable sources. For these and other reasons, critical and honest self-appraisals thrive in an environment in which intellectual curiosity and truth-seeking drives the process, and stakeholders contribute based on their expertise rather than on their position. They also require the utility of foresight and anticipation to inform adaptation.

Some of our case studies raise the question of how intense and immediate this self-reflection must be to drive meaningful reform. In the British case, the evidence of social troubles was obvious in the filthy and smog-bound streets, cholera outbreaks, and labor unrest. The number and seriousness of social ills contributed to a relatively urgent sense, on the part of many reformers, that the alternative to change was serious instability. Despite Britain's self-perceptions, it took decades for gradual change to be pushed through. In other cases, the appreciation of the need for change may be less intense and insufficient to overcome political obstacles to reform.

Some political systems may be more capable of self-diagnosis than others. National self-diagnoses tend to be associated with open, democratic societies that feature the free exchange of ideas, though they have not been exclusive to democratic forms of governance alone. In the mid-19th century, for example, Japanese leaders were confronted with overwhelming Western economic and military power and recognized that they had fallen behind. Absent a decisive transformation, Japan would not have been able to reap the fruits of the scientific and industrial revolutions. Japanese leaders opened their country's doors and began importing and adapting Western ideas and methods in education, technology, production, the military, and even fashion.[5]

In the field of political science, the literature on epistemic communities discusses how problems, such as climate change or trade policy, necessitate the development of new sciences or knowledge to address them.[6] The freedom enjoyed by expert groups in a society to reflect on these issues—typically exercised by researchers with academic freedom and potentially bolstered by a free press to stimulate open debate—is instrumental in addressing potential economic, technological, environmental, or political sources of decline and advance solutions. Without this latitude to engage in solution-seeking, which potentially goes against the interests of those who benefit from the status quo, unsatisfactory changes are ineffective at addressing root problems.

---

[5] Kenichi Ohno, "Meiji Japan: Progressive Learning of Western Technology," in Arkebe Oqubay and Kenichi Ohno, eds., *How Nations Learn: Technological Learning, Industrial Policy, and Catch-Up*, Oxford University Press, 2019.

[6] Peter M. Haas, "Policy Knowledge: Epistemic Communities," in Neil J. Smelser and Paul B. Baltes, eds., *International Encyclopedia of Social and Behavioral Sciences*, Pergamon, 2001; William T. Drake and Kalypso Nicolaidis, "Ideas, Interests, and Institutionalism: 'Trade in Services' and the Uruguay Round," *International Organization*, Vol. 46, No. 1, 1992; Clair Gough and Simon Shackley, "The Respectable Politics of Climate Change: The Epistemic Communities and NGOs," *International Affairs*, Vol. 77, No. 2, April 2001.

Accurate Diagnosis of the Challenges

The case studies we examined highlight a second criterion for national renewal: an accurate sense of what the problem is and, therefore, the scope of necessary solutions. In the British and U.S. cases, social reformers, including national leaders, rightly identified a clear set of social ills, ranging from working conditions and inequality to the lack of a complete franchise and the need for improved institutions of governance. This self-diagnosis led to elements of a response, which—although not necessarily designed together as a coherent strategy (and sometimes spread out over years or even decades)—helped to prompt renewal by addressing the true sources of the decline.

In contrast, an inaccurate or unclear diagnosis leads to misplaced cures. In the Soviet case, Gorbachev and other leaders had a sense of the symptoms of stagnation and decay but did not begin the reform process with a clear sense of their causes. They focused more on experimenting with various policy initiatives in the hope of jump-starting growth and other forms of dynamism but did so almost in isolation from the true sources of the problem. As a result, they convinced themselves that they could reverse the USSR's decline without tackling core issues, such as spending on subsidies, which ultimately broke the budget.

A Problem-Solving Mindset

Recognizing the value of introspection and foresight must be matched by a dedicated focus on improvement—a problem-solving mindset, which is our second factor of renewal. It is the natural complement to recognizing the need for change in laying the basis for renewal.

The evidence for the importance of a problem-solving mindset derives from sources similar to those that espouse the value of introspection. In both of the deeper case studies, British and U.S. political, business, and social leaders displayed a drive to solve the problems they had identified, a drive that was essential to the renewal sparked in both cases. The absence of such drive is a leading characteristic of several of the theories of decline listed in Chapter 4, particularly those that involve weakening national willpower alongside a predominant attitude of satisfaction and entitlement. The societal characteristics of national ambition and willpower, as well as a problem-solving mindset, speak to a kind of responsive and active determination to identify and solve social and economic problems.

The resulting motivation speaks to broader societal traits regarding worldview and work ethos. Such societal traits as industriousness, discipline, and a focus on improving the here and now, relate to a society's ability to renew.[7] Such a worldview includes a general concern with the future rather than with the present, with production rather than consumption, and with the practical rather than the metaphysical.[8]

In achieving this sort of adaptation and responsiveness, the nexus between scientific research—whether basic or applied—and real-world problems is of paramount importance. While Great Britain's eclipse of the Netherlands as the world's leading great power in the late-17th century certainly relied on its resources and size,[9] a key factor was Britain's emphasis on the practical rather than the metaphysical. In the 17th and 18th centuries, research in Great Britain centered on physics and engineering sciences rather than arcane theological debates. In the Netherlands (and in continental Europe more generally), theology and philosophy dominated instead. Margaret Jacob wrote

> [b]y contrast, in the library of the academy of Hardewijk, where the new science is very much in evidence during the second half of the

---

[7] Making that point with reference to the Dutch case, see Albert Hyma, "Calvinism and Capitalism in the Netherlands, 1555–1700," *Journal of Modern History*, Vol. 10, No. 3, 1938.

[8] Simon Schama refers to the Dutch merchants' relentless focus on improving their material situation combined with prudent political stewardship of the Netherlands' rising economic clout, as captured by the epitome "I invest, he speculates, they gamble." See Simon Schama, *The Embarrassment of Riches: An Interpretation of Dutch Culture in the Golden Age*, Fontana Press, 1987, p. 343.

[9] Stephen Broadberry, Bruce M. S. Campbell, Alexander Klein, Mark Overton, and Bas van Leeuwen, "Britain in an International Context," in *British Economic Growth, 1270–1870*, Cambridge University Press, 2015, pp. 395–396. Pomeranz argues for the combination of the scientific mindset, instruments, and resources. See Kenneth Pomeranz, *The Great Divergence: China, Europe, and the Making of the World Economy*, Princeton University Press, 2000, pp. 66–69.

seventeenth century, emphasis in the eighteenth century appears to have been legal, medical, and theological, rather than scientific or mechanical. . . . Only very late in the eighteenth century do we begin to see evidence in the province of Gelderland for the existence of public scientific lecturing intended for commerce, trade, and industry. . . . A similar lack of interest in science also plagued the academy at Deventer, and progressive parents in turn sent their children elsewhere on the Continent or to Amsterdam, where by the 1760s public agitation for reform in scientific education began in earnest.[10]

This difference meant that Cartesian thinkers on the Continent busied themselves with questions of a more metaphysical nature whose answers did not yield any concrete applications. Meanwhile, on the other side of the English Channel, science and engineering blossomed as British thinkers not only deciphered the laws of nature but also developed a cumulative body of knowledge to create applications that dealt with real-world problems.[11] The research of figures such as Robert Boyle (gas), Isaac Newton (gravity), James Watt (electricity), and James Prescott Joule (energy) yielded insights and applications that contributed to growing mastery over nature.

This pattern recurs throughout different periods in history. Long before the Scientific Revolution and especially during its Golden Age (the eighth and ninth centuries), the Abbasid Caliphate fostered tremendous progress in mathematics, cartography, architecture, and infrastructure through its focus on science to solve challenges.[12] More recently, South Korea's transformation from a poor, developing nation in the early 1960s to the economic and technological powerhouse it is at the time of this writing would not have been possible without a persistent pursuit of progress rather than happiness. As great powers mature and reach their peak, a combination of structural

---

[10] Margaret C. Jacob, *The Cultural Meaning of the Scientific Revolution*, Temple University Press, 1988, p. 189.

[11] Jack A. Goldstone, "Efflorescences and Economic Growth in World History: Rethinking the 'Rise of the West' and the Industrial Revolution," *Journal of World History*, Vol. 13, No. 2, Fall 2002, pp. 367–373.

[12] For an overview, see Ahmet T. Kuru, *Islam, Authoritarianism, and Underdevelopment: A Global and Historical Comparison*, Cambridge University Press, 2019, Chapter 4.

factors start inhibiting their pursuit of progress. These cases and others suggest that recognizing challenges and an appreciation for solving these challenges through practical action are required to reignite national dynamism.

The case studies we reviewed suggest that the resulting problem-solving mindset must ultimately produce—or be grounded in—some degree of national consensus on the broad direction of change: in other words, a collective judgment on the necessity of change and some degree of its nature. In the British case, the Great Exhibition of 1851 and its advocate Prince Albert's broader role in pushing new ways of thinking and investments in technological progress reflected both an applied and adaptive mindset, as well as an openness to new ways of thinking.[13] In the U.S. case, both leading parties eventually shared some commitment to populist or progressive reform to share wealth more equitably and rein in the increasingly dominant power of monopolies after the Gilded Age. In Meiji Japan, the need for industrialization became a widely shared consensus. A national problem-solving mindset may be ineffectual if an ideologically and politically fragmented context leads to disagreement about the direction that change should take.

Support for innovation and experimentation—the resources to fund such explorations, the legal or regulatory environment that empowers them, and the absence of orthodoxies that prevent them—is an important component of this factor in national renewal. Furthermore, it requires an intellectual atmosphere that tolerates criticism of the status quo. In modern cases, it also demands significant investments in research and development and a wide variety of experiments to test new techniques or technologies.

Multiple and Overlapping Efforts to Solve Distinct Challenges

The fourth variable related to national renewal emerges largely from our two in-depth case studies, which suggest that decline in great powers is typically multicausal and expressed through various symptoms. Any process of

---

[13] Simon Heffer, *High Minds: The Victorians and the Birth of Modern Britain*, Pegasus Books, 2022, pp. 285–339.

renewal will therefore have to involve marshaling resources to address the manifold facets of a decline.

Partly because of the multiple sources of stagnation, national renewal efforts generally consist of mosaics of campaigns, initiatives, and strategies rather than unified, top-down mandates. The two major case studies clearly reflect this pattern. Victorian-era Britain witnesses a whole series of reform movements on different issues, including child labor, women's suffrage, and environmental standards. Though seldom formally linked, they were responding to some of the same broad conceptions of national crisis and eventually contributed to a shared sense of progress and renewal.

The same pattern emerged in the U.S. Progressive era. As noted above, the Progressive movement was made up of a variety of political actors and interests with an array of high-priority goals. Activist groups, progressive business leaders, and politicians targeted different issues, from better pay and working conditions to antitrust and anti-corruption law. Because many of these themes came to reside under the umbrella of the Progressive Party, the response was arguably somewhat more unified than in Victorian-era Britain. However, the diverse factions that made up this party were sometimes at odds; in many ways, this process of responding to multiple national challenges was just as much a series of issue-specific initiatives as it was in the British case.

One broader theme or quality that links several of these characteristics together is a collective focus on the future. A drive for national renewal requires a sense of future-orientation, a belief that the future can be better than the present, and that hard work and carefully planning can realize that future. Empirical research has suggested that a society's orientation to time is a critical variable in shaping its developmental trajectory,[14] and this basic sense of intentionality and future orientation is related to many of the characteristics of renewal.

Therefore, one lesson of our research is that, while development can be top-down in some cases, renewal from a position of established strength must be grassroots and pluralistic—at least to some degree—to achieve its intended effects.

---

[14] For example, see the multiple references to time in Harrison and Huntington, 2000.

Capable Governance Structures and Social Institutions

The general literature on sources of national rise and decline, the case studies, and the first phase of our research have led us to identify a fifth contributing factor to prospective national renewal: Effective governance structures and social institutions capable of execution and oversight. Separate from the ability of a society to diagnose problems and research solutions, institutions must be capable of implementing and sustaining measures to stave or reverse decline. State capacity to oversee governance operations, reduce the transactional costs of conducting business, enforce state laws, and protect lives and property effectively, efficiently, and with legitimacy is key to initiating and continuing efforts through periods of decline.[15] Without the ability to carry out the basic governance or the potentially more-complicated measures necessary to realize solutions (such as establishing or expanding social welfare, carrying out complex regulatory schemes, or developing and leveraging technological fields), efforts to address the core causes and symptoms of declines may fail—even if they are correct in terms of their methods and aims.

Elite Commitment to the Common Good

A sixth factor important for national renewal is the indispensable role of elite commitment. This is the theme of another report in this project series, which describes the nature of a public-spirited elite and its importance to national dynamism and competitive advantage.[16] Our research uncovered an interesting fact: Although they were explored by different researchers, the case studies that emerged for renewed dynamism overlapped signifi-

---

[15] Matthew Adam Kocher, "State Capacity as a Conceptual Variable," *Yale Journal of International Affairs*, Vol. 5, No. 2, 2010, pp. 137–145. While our discussion of state capacity here is general, we mean to highlight the multifaceted ways that a state can have the capacity to carry out a number of functions (e.g., the capacity to collect taxes).

[16] Michael J. Mazarr, Daniel Tapia, Anton Shenk, William Anthony Hay, Geoffrey Kabaservice, Zongyuan Zoe Liu, *Public-Spirited Elites and National Fates*, RAND Corporation, RR-A2611-4, forthcoming.

cantly with the cases of public-spirited elites: such as 1930s–1960s United States, Victorian-era Britain, and Meiji Japan.[17] This parallelism highlights the connection between an elite committed to the common good and successful national renewal.

Various authors have stressed the important contribution of elite commitment to sustained or repeated competitive success. Oswald Spengler singled out Roman families as the source of a talented elite that might not have had any constitutionally established status, but "found its constitutional engine in the Senate";[18] these elites allowed Rome to thrive for many centuries before falling prey to state capture. Paul Kennedy pointed to the British elites' commitment to public service and the acumen with which they balanced domestic reform, economic growth, and international expansion.[19] If economic elites abandon public service and will not sacrifice for their country, the state no longer has their resources to draw on for reforms during trying times. As Simon Heffer noted, industrialization and growing riches in the Victorian era "pricked the consciences of those enriched by it. An intellectual elite sought to . . . drive movements for reform in education, housing, public health, the law and the constitution."[20]

National renewal and elite commitment are related for various reasons. One is effective governance: It is essential that political and economic elites take pride in public service and continue to serve the res publica even after the initial spoils of empire have been harvested. Following the initial rise of many great powers, there is a marked increase in rent-seeking behavior in which state budgets are channeled to unproductive ventures while the upkeep of state administrative structures requires ever larger means,

---

[17] Although we did not examine it in detail, the case of Prussia (Germany) also strongly supports the role of a public-spirited elite in underwriting national renewal in ways ranging from support for research and education to military service and emphasis on a meritocracy with service to the nation as its core value. See the discussion in Peter Watson, *The German Genius: Europe's Third Renaissance, the Second Scientific Revolution, and the Twentieth Century*, HarperCollins, 2010.

[18] In the words of Adda B. Bozeman, "Decline of the West? Spengler Reconsidered," *Virginia Quarterly Review*, Spring 1983.

[19] Kennedy, 1989.

[20] Heffer, 2022, p. xvi.

which happened both to the Spanish (late-16th to early-17th century) and the Ottoman Empires (late-19th to early-20th century). This trend is often exaccrbated by state capture by private interests, which translates into lower taxes, subsidies, or tariff protection for business elites.[21] It is further reinforced by an unwillingness of the best and brightest to serve in public administration roles.

A second causal link stresses the role of public-spirited elites in underwriting social cohesion. Self-interested, rent-seeking elites create conditions for populist upheavals that can destabilize societies and bring to power undemocratic or self-destructive leaders. They also create the conditions for a public loss of faith in governing myths, narratives, and institutions, which undermines the ability of a society to compete and achieve influence from the power of its example.

Participation in an Era's Core Model of Value Creation

Beyond the initiation of a national-renewal movement and a state and society's capacity to carry it out, renewal also requires that a state is in sync with the new era's core model of value creation, which is the seventh factor associated with national renewal. This is especially true since the industrial revolution but was arguably also true before it. A state needs to be either a frontrunner or, at least, in alignment with that core model of value creation to reignite a period of sustained growth and competitiveness. Another paper in this project series makes this argument directly by surveying paradigms of competitive success and the ways in which nations that have aligned themselves to their era's demands increase their odds of renewal.[22] A nation

---

[21] Goldstone argues that historically this has been a natural process: Following a period of innovation and growth, new equilibria came into place in which "economic and political elites sought to defend existing social patterns. Such inertial states were prone to decay . . . and the collapse of complexly interwoven economic and political structures" (Goldstone, 2002, p. 378).

[22] Michael J. Mazarr, Alexis Dale-Huang, and Matthew Sargent, *The Emerging Competitive Paradigm: A Contest of Effective Governance*, RAND Corporation, PE-A2611-1, February 2024.

can satisfy many preconditions of renewal, but if its society and economy are fatally misaligned to the demands of the competitive paradigm, it will face powerful barriers to success.

Both phases of our research offer many clear-cut examples of this relationship. An early case is 16th-century Netherlands and its financial innovations to sustain far-flung overseas trade networks.[23] Great Britain's mastery of the early industrial revolution and the later industrial muscle of the United States, Germany, and Japan are more-recent examples, as is the United States' leadership in both software and hardware application, which led to Silicon Valley's boom from 1980s and 1990s onward.

The importance of a nation's timeliness with value creation also relates to the essential role of international legitimacy to national renewal. This is partly because of the power and dynamism that came out of international networks, which will be denied to countries lacking legitimacy. The Soviet case is especially telling in this regard. Moscow knew it needed access to international science, technology, investment, and talent. Therefore, it undertook a series of peace offensives—culminating in the détente of the 1970s and the Gorbachev revolution of the 1980s—while trying to cover up the grim reality of Soviet life. These tendencies were apparent as early as 1957 when the USSR hosted the World Youth Festival. Renewal and international opprobrium do not mix.

Sustainable Access to Essential Resources for Renewal (Financial and Material)

Finally, our research and the two cases we have reviewed in more detail have led us to identify an eighth factor as critical to campaigns of national renewal: Financial and other state resources are necessary to accomplish renewal tasks in a sustainable way. Efforts at renewal can be expensive propositions, requiring investment in an array of technologies, institutions, or

---

[23] See Kennedy, 1989, pp. 77–79. For a critical, in-depth assessment, see Jan de Vries and Ad Van Der Woude, *The First Modern Economy: Success, Failure, and Perseverance of the Dutch Economy, 1500–1815*, Cambridge University Press, 1997, especially pp. 129–158.

programs, ranging from social insurance and military technology to basic science and national infrastructure. Both in the Victorian and Progressive era cases, Britain and the United States made significant investments in a variety of components of their renewal strategies. These investments included social programs, infrastructure, military capabilities, and more. In contrast, the Soviet effort at renewal was hamstrung by insufficient resources to undertake the most important reforms, such as price adjustments.

One important aspect of this resource issue is the material capacity of great powers and how those sources evolve over time. The importance of reliable financial and material resources is essential to national renewal and is a theme that emerges from the cases we reviewed. Victorian-era Britain continued to expropriate wealth from its colonies, which helped sustain its resource base and thus contributed to its renewal. The United States had only emerged from the conquest of the frontier, which is generally held to have been completed just after 1890, and was about to embark on its own temporary burst of formal colonial acquisition. In other cases, such as that of Habsburg Spain, the loss of empire denuded the crown of vast stores of precious metals, which were essential to its power. This analysis does not have the space to deeply investigate the role of external resources in fostering renewal, but they clearly complement the domestic elements we highlight in the cases. Importantly, too, nations can take internal steps to shift their resource situation through conservation, by updating its sources of energy and materials, innovation, and more.

CHAPTER 7

Lessons for the United States

Our analysis has been suggestive and exploratory rather than definitive. As we have noted, history does not offer lessons that are simple or necessarily transferable regarding the challenge of national renewal. However, the historical record does support several of our preliminary findings.

First, *recovery from significant long-term national decline is rare and difficult to detect in the historical record.* When great powers have slid from a position of preeminence or leadership because of domestic factors, they have seldom reversed this trend. Some cases of partial decline do not appear as a comprehensive national fall because there was a timely and successful process of anticipatory renewal.

Second, *the United States may be entering a period requiring the kind of anticipatory national renewal that we find in several historical cases.* In Britain and the United States (and likely in other cases that we did not review in depth), these societies identified challenges to their dynamism and competitive position and undertaken broad-based social, political, and economic reforms to sustain their power. They had not yet declined significantly (if at all) when these processes began, and it is not clear how severely their competitiveness would have otherwise suffered. However, the risk of more rapid decline was clear, and the reform and renewal efforts very likely underwrote continued relative power for decades if not longer.

Table 3.1, which summarized the causal connections between societal characteristics and national renewal, points to a critical moment for the United States at the time of writing. In successful cases of anticipatory renewal, negative trends in many of those areas—including national unity and willpower, shared opportunity, a learning and adapting mindset, and effective active states and institutions—threatened national competitiveness. However, those trends were at least partly arrested because of reform agendas. At the time of writing, the United States seems to have arrived at a similar moment when a variety of challenges may have serious effects on national dynamism and the potential for renewal. We may already have slid further in a negative direction than Victorian-era Britain or the United States during the Gilded Age. The urgency of response is clear.

Third, *several common factors appear to distinguish cases of successful anticipatory renewal from failures.* As noted above, we assessed the historical record and our three primary cases in light of our preliminary research and the seven major societal characteristics associated with competitive success. Table 7.1 lists major factors associated with successful and failed anticipatory renewal.

Fourth, the United States does not yet appear to be demonstrating widespread shared recognition of societal challenges or the determination to reform and change in key issue areas. In this sense, it has not yet reached the position of Britain in the 1840s and 1850s or the United States after the 1890s, which both witnessed a surge of generalized reform to address multiple social challenges that resulted in broad-based national renewal. The United States does not yet have a shared recognition of the problem: While some challenges are generating widespread frustration, there is no emerging consensus on the barriers to renewal that demand urgent action. The

TABLE 7.1

Comparing Attributes of Anticipatory Renewal Versus Decline

Successful Anticipatory Renewal (Britain, United States)	Failed Renewal or Steady Decline (Soviet Union and Others)
• Sense of national solidarity and commitment to common project • Multiple actors throughout society identifying and seeking to mitigate challenges—especially a critical mass of elites • Society in general and governments in particular with sufficient resources to deploy reforms • Reform groups having a clear understanding of problems and feasible solutions to promote	• Weak collective identity, no commitment to common project, and waning national willpower • Some social actors recognize problems but are vigorously opposed by others defending their interests; elites fractured or self-interested • Public and private sectors have strict limits on resources they can bring to bear • Leading social actors either have little or differ widely in their understanding of the sources of societal problems; no coherent action plan

SOURCE: This table synthesizes conclusions from the analyses presented in Chapter 5.

essential problem is seen in starkly different terms by different segments of society and groups of political leaders. This lack of a common vision creates a distinct challenge for the multiple efforts, which are a typical hallmark of periods of national renewal, to solve key issues: As a result, opportunity may not emerge. Table 7.2 offers a very brief assessment of where the United States stands in each of the major areas required for anticipatory renewal.

This analysis highlights the particular threat posed by the combination of a ruined information environment, political polarization and fragmentation, and objective evidence that institutions of governance are seizing up and losing public confidence. Taken together, those intersecting trends could demoralize this sort of grassroots, generalized process of national renewal.

We would also highlight the importance of adaptive governing institutions capable of shepherding the United States through the demands of the emerging era. In another paper in this series, we stressed the importance of the competitive paradigm of a given period.[1] Nations that aligned themselves to the requirements of their era—such as those that became industrial powerhouses during the second industrial revolution—gained tremendous advantage. We argued that the defining feature of the next competitive paradigm will be effective and innovative governance.

Finally, we reach a more optimistic finding: *The United States has all the preconditions for a potential agenda of anticipatory renewal.* It is not consigned by international politics to further relative decline, especially regarding China (which has its own problems in all of these areas). The United States is not in the position of the USSR in the 1980s. It has tremendous residual strengths and a proven capacity for resilience and renewal. It has the scale and industrial and scientific foundations to remain one of the great powers at the apex of world politics. It has a rich reservoir of social actors capable of conducting the same sort of campaign for reform and renewal that occurred in Victorian-era Britain and turn-of-the-20th-century United States.

Many powerful barriers stand in the way of a process of national renewal. They include a poisoned information environment, deep and seemingly entrenched political polarization, and an elite class that has not yet dem-

---

[1] Mazarr, Dale-Huang, and Sargent, 2024.

TABLE 7.2
Requirements for National Renewal and the Current U.S. Case

Requirement	Evidence and Indicators	U.S. Status in 2024
Recognition of the problem	• Public debates, analysis of social issues, and challenges • Shared agreement on at least a handful of core problems • Expression of this agreement in political terms, such as legislative groups and activist organizations	**Mixed:** Very widespread discussion of many social challenges but sharp disagreements over their causes and the priorities between various social and economic issues; no coherent vision of what ails the society; a variety of political activist organizations but often in direct opposition on key issues; this factor could be more advanced on the state level.
Accurate diagnosis of the challenges	• Public discussions and analyses that focus attention on key issues • Leadership prioritization of most important issues based on diagnosis	**Present but not shared:** Diagnoses of challenges to national renewal litter the public sphere, but diagnoses tend to be partisan, and there is no critical mass of leaders with a unified view; specific interest groups identify narrower issues but gain only limited traction because they cannot generate a broad consensus.
Problem-solving mindset	• Focus on practical solutions to problems rather than partisan or ideological gain • Emphasis on seeking best practices and sharing approaches to solving problems	**Mixed:** Highly uneven across social institutions and governing levels; strongly present in some states and localities; reservoirs in Congress and executive agencies; reflected in commitment to reform many nongovernmental organizations (NGOs) and public-private endeavors; not consistent and blocked in many cases by polarization; lack of consensus on needed steps; other factors.
Multiple and overlapping efforts to solve distinct challenges	• Emergence of strong activist or interest groups pushing specific changes or reforms on one or small set of issues • Support for such movements from a critical mass of elites and political leaders	**Mixed but potentially improving:** The overall social pattern still does not match that of the Victorian or Progressive era mosaics of reform, but many efforts have begun in states, localities, NGOs, and elsewhere; foundation is in place for expanded efforts that would begin to create real momentum.

Table 7.2—Continued

Requirement	Evidence and Indicators	U.S. Status in 2024
Capable governance structures and social institutions	• Transparent and effective public bureaucracies • Working legislatures generating bipartisan responses to national problems • Effective NGOs from charities to business alliances devoted to the common good	**Mixed:** The essential institutional quality of public and private sectors remains reasonably strong on many counts, especially at the state and local levels, but there are critical problems (for example, the relative impotence of Congress and the stifling bureaucracy in many areas of federal and even state administrations); the result is exceedingly low levels of public faith in these institutions.
Elite commitment to the common good	• Elite participation in the public sector and military service • Levels of elite philanthropy • Participation in shared public life (e.g., housing, civic organizations) • Business leader support for limits to corporate power • Role in leading, supporting, or endorsing reform movements or on specific issues	**Weak but uncertain:** Measures of elite participation in shared elements of national life definitely in decline; philanthropy arguably stagnating or declining (overall numbers held up by some mega-gifts); some signs of renewed commitment to reforms of common interest but many signs of generalized focus on self-interest.
Participation in the era's leading model for value creation	• Advanced industries in frontier technology areas • Human capital and institutional capacity to participate in leading industries, advanced warfare, and other aspects of prevailing competitive paradigm	**Strong but threatened:** U.S. industries remain highly competitive in leading technology areas and frontier industries; the United States has strong multinational ties with other leading industrial nations; however, emerging value creation model depends critically on a recovery of the quality of governance; and the United States has clear shortcomings in this area.[a]

Table 7.2—Continued

Requirement	Evidence and Indicators	U.S. Status in 2024
Sustainable access to essential resources for renewal (financial and material)	• Sufficient financial basis to underwrite ambitions of the state • Access to nonfinancial resources required for economic and military strength	**Weak:** The United States has significant and intensifying fiscal constraints on major national investments and is dependent on other countries for critical resources (such as technology components and rare earth materials).

[a] For more on this subject, see Mazarr, Dale-Huang, and Sargent, 2024.

onstrated the sort of widespread commitment to the common good of earlier eras. In one sense, the United States is ideally poised to undertake yet another of its repeated eras of reform and renewal, one that would fortify U.S. social and political stability and strengthen the roots of its global power. The question is whether, at the beginning of the 21st century, the United States confronts new and deadly threats to the solidarity, understanding, and commitment necessary for another round of national renewal.

Case Study: Victorian-Era Great Britain

We conducted four case studies of attempted national renewal to derive lessons for the United States at the time of writing. These are Victorian-era Britain, Progressive-era United States, late–Cold War Soviet Union, and the British and U.S. attempts at renewal during the 1970s and 1980s. We specifically sought cases that were not simply postwar recovery programs (for example, Germany and Japan, or even France, after World War II) or programs of modernization (such as Meiji Japan). Rather, we identified two cases in which a nation confronted significant threats to its influence and competitiveness and undertook a program of renewal to mitigate those risks. This and the following appendix summarize these cases.

The British case offers one of the most significant examples of a great power becoming aware of dangerous trends potentially affecting its global standing and undertaking many policy initiatives and reforms to extend its geopolitical influence for several decades. In the long run, Great Britain was destined to slide into a secondary position in global power rankings because of its limited size, its gradual loss of colonial income and reach, and the dramatic rise of massive great powers (including the United States, to a degree Germany, and eventually the Soviet Union and China) which surged past Britain through industrialization. This was partly Britain's fault: The post-1945 narrative is largely one of British decline and inability to keep pace with the industrial, technological, and social power of other leading nations. But the period examined in this case, from roughly the 1820s through the end of the 19th century, was one of at least temporary renewal.

Simon Heffer catalogued much of this process in his magisterial book *High Minds*. He contends that

> [i]n the four decades between the rise of political consciousness that manifested itself in Chartism, and the return of William Ewart Gladstone to Downing Street in 1880 . . . British life changed almost beyond recognition. Although poverty, disease, ignorance, squalor and injustice were far from eliminated, they were beaten back more in those forty or so years than at any previous time in the history of Britain.[1]

He explains that this was partly because "[a] sense of earnest, disinterested moral purpose distinguished many politicians, intellectuals and citizens of mid-nineteenth-century Britain, and drove them to seek to improve the condition of the whole of society."[2] How this process evolved, as well as the degree to which it underwrote at least a temporary surge of national renewal, was the focus of this case.

The process of social and economic reform was not universally altruistic. Although it was pushed by some progressive social reformers, it also resulted from the fact that expanding suffrage forced political parties to appeal to the interests of the working class and the desire to maintain British competitiveness as a great power. Reform was slow and uneven: These efforts did not forestall long-term relative decline or even the later "British disease" of economic and productivity stagnation. Nevertheless, these efforts allowed Britain to avoid worse outcomes and revitalize its position as a leading great power, especially after 1850.

The following narrative focuses on domestic developments within Great Britain that helped to shape its competitive position. While the costs and benefits of being the world's leading imperial power were significant in determining Britain's competitive position, its imperial resources were not necessarily responsible for the *renewal* of British power in the late 19th century. Instead, our focus is on domestic trends that help to explain Britain's social, political, and economic renewal, which also arguably sustained its imperial power.

---

[1]   Heffer, 2022, p. xiii.

[2]   Heffer, 2022, p. xiii.

Risks of Decline

At the end of the Napoleonic Wars in 1815, Britain remained "lightly governed by a Pittite landed elite."[3] Britain had just led a coalition to defeat the greatest Continental power, in part with the aid of the world's dominant navy, and looked set for a long period of geopolitical primacy. In a larger sense, since the late 17th century, Britain had grown "from a second-rank nation on the periphery of the Continent into a great power whose wealth, stability and liberty were the envy of Europe."[4] However, as Britain strengthened its role as the world's leading industrial power over the next two decades, British society was afflicted with a set of interconnected ills that risked undermining its dynamism, stability, and, ultimately, national power.

The process of reform and renewal began with a set of interlocking recognitions that British social and political life faced a series of challenges, which had to be addressed if the nation was going to preserve its harmony and stability, as well as its global predominance.[5] This discussion was reflected in the famous "Condition of England Question," which was raised by multiple social critics, including Thomas Carlyle and Frederick Engels, who pushed these issues to the forefront of public debate. This theme was also strongly reflected in the era's fiction, including in Dickens' oeuvre and Elizabeth Gaskell's *Mary Barton*.

Many British citizens and political observers founded their criticisms on a sense of dishonesty and political stagnation in a political system commonly termed "Old Corruption." This perception was somewhat exaggerated: Even before 1820, reforms had emphasized merit and reined in the use of government for corrupt purposes.[6] However, the view that government—including the monarchy—did not serve the people was widespread and was already generating protests throughout the country.

---

[3] Miles Taylor, "Review: British Politics in the Age of Revolution and Reform, 1789–1867," *Historical Journal*, Vol. 45, No. 3, September 2002, p. 662.

[4] Correlli Barnett, *The Collapse of British Power*, Eyre Methuen, 1972, p. 20.

[5] Bentley B. Gilbert, *The Evolution of National Insurance in Great Britain: The Origins of the Welfare State*, Michael Joseph, 1966, p. 13.

[6] Susie L. Steinbach, *Understanding the Victorians: Politics, Culture, and Society in Nineteenth-Century Britain*, 3rd ed., Routledge Press, 2023, pp. 37–38, 41.

The effects of industrialization on worker and environmental conditions also contributed to a sense of unease. Workers toiled for long hours in awful conditions for miserable pay. Many of them were children: As late as 1851, 180,000 children worked in the textile industry and 38,000 children worked in mines.[7] For many reformers, "[t]he backdrop to this drama is a scene of grim factory towns with overworked children, squalid slums, and unsightly mills."[8] Reformers were "alarmed at the cruelty of life in factory towns" and held "a vision of an organic, benevolent society, which will remove cruelty and ugliness and neglect."[9] The 19th century saw a significant and rising concern for the conditions of Britain's working class.

Furthermore, as Simon Heffer notes, Britain was "beset by terrible, and destabilising, social problems," in the 1830s, which included cholera outbreaks and an absence of medical care for the poor. "Food was unnecessarily expensive because of import tariffs, and often adulterated or diseased; and water unsafe to drink. . . . The destitute lived in workhouses where families were broken up. . . . Women were the property of their husbands. Only a small proportion of adult men could vote."[10] The 1834 Poor Law Amendment Act was not so much an effort to avoid destitution as it was to stigmatize and criminalize the condition based on the firm aristocratic conviction that public aid would undermine the effective operation of the labor market.[11] With rising social unrest, obvious poverty, and a seeming drift in the direction of worse outcomes, many observers increasingly felt the need for reform through the 1840s.

---

[7] Michael Levin, *The Condition of England Question: Carlyle, Mill, Engels*, St. Martin's Press, 1998, p. 19.

[8] David Roberts, "Tory Paternalism and Social Reform in Early Victorian England," *American Historical Review*, Vol. 63, No. 2, January 1958, pp. 323–324.

[9] Roberts, 1958, p. 324.

[10] Heffer, 2022, p. xv.

[11] Anthony Brundage, "Reform of the Poor Law Electoral System, 1834–94," *Albion: A Quarterly Journal Concerned with British Studies*, Vol. 7, No. 3, 1975; Thomas Nutt, "Illegitimacy, Paternal Financial Responsibility, and the 1834 Poor Law Commission Report: The Myth of the Old Poor Law and the Making of the New," *Economic History Review*, Vol. 63, No. 2, 2010.

It is important not to exaggerate how comprehensive this recognition was or how quickly it emerged during the Victorian era. As late as 1870, the London *Times* editorialized that "[w]e can . . . look on the present with undisturbed satisfaction. Our commerce is extending and multiplying its world-wide ramifications without much regard for the croaking of any political or scientific Cassandras. . . . Turn where we may, we find in our commerce no traces of decadence."[12] Many leading figures in British society did not share any sense of imminent crisis and opposed many proposed reforms. Elements of the aristocracy fought certain reforms hard; it took years to repeal the Corn Laws, even once the real push was underway. The process of reform and renewal took so long in Britain in part because it reflected a long series of battles between those who appreciated the need for change and were willing to undertake painful adaptations and those who did not feel that same urgency.

Reform did push forward, in part because it was driven by the self-interest of the elites, the wealthy, and the powerful. Without change, many began to appreciate (educated in part by recurring labor unrest) "the affluence of the few might well have been destroyed by the revolution of the masses."[13] The chastening example of the French Revolution was not yet ancient history by the Victorian era. There was a sense that serious social and political instability was entirely plausible and that gradual reform was a far preferable option. Changes in voting rights law accelerated other reforms: Writing of the Poor Law, for example, one scholar concludes that "[a] system of public relief deliberately made hideous for its recipients could not long outlast the grant of universal franchise."[14] Without attention to working-class interests, those classes "would eventually displace the traditional parties with a party of their own."[15]

By the middle of the 19th century, therefore, those opposed to reform were increasingly on the defensive. After 1842, Heffer explains, "[t]hose

---

[12] Quoted in Robert F. Haggard, *The Persistence of Victorian Liberalism: The Politics of Social Reform in Britain, 1870–1900*, Greenwood Press, 2001, pp. 13–14.

[13] Heffer, 2022, p. 1.

[14] Gilbert, 1966, p. 15.

[15] Gilbert, 1966, p. 59.

with a vision of change were about to have the upper hand," and by about 1880, "the forces of reaction were largely burnt out," overcome by objective evidence of the need for change from grinding poverty to "the increasingly angry, organised and large protests of those who wanted the vote."[16] The "condition of the people," as it was referred to, was now an unavoidable part of British politics.

The Agenda of Reform

As it unfolded in the 1840s, that vision of change would end up having several leading components. However, a critical aspect of this process was that it took decades to play out, and the eventual success of the drive was in doubt throughout the whole process. Susie Steinbach has organized the reform drive into three main periods: an early phase from 1820 to 1850, which saw "the extension of the franchise to most middle-class men" and a broadly more comprehensive and professionalized national political scene; a middle phase running roughly from 1850 to the mid-1880s, which saw reforms in areas of corruption and further expanded the vote; and a final period from the 1880s through World War I, which witnessed the passage of social insurance and other reforms but also labor unrest and a constitutional crisis.[17]

Throughout these years, the drive for national renewal was a bottom-up—not top-down—process. Comparisons of British and German drives for reform and renewal in the 19th century document how Britain's effort was broad-based, grounded in private organizations and philanthropy, with distinct coalitions and interests backing very different pieces of reform across half a century, often for different reasons. It certainly included critical pieces of legislation and governmental initiatives, but they did not dominate the effort. In contrast, reform in Germany was state-centric.[18] If anything, the British case reflects "the very lack of a defined reforming agenda

---

[16] Heffer, 2022, pp. 49, 378; Gilbert, 1966, pp. 18–19.

[17] Steinbach, 2023, p. 35.

[18] Eckhart Hellmuth, ed., *The Transformation of Political Culture: England and Germany in the Late Eighteenth Century*, Oxford University Press, 1990; T. C. W. Blanning

and a preference instead for timely adaptation" as opposed to a carefully structured and administered plan of renewal.[19]

Although the decades-long process of reform was not undertaken with a specifically religious purpose—and, indeed, some reformers saw it as their purpose to ease the influence of religion on daily life—many reformers were inspired by a moral sensibility grounded in their Christian faith.[20] This reflected a search for nobility and self-perfection that defined the era, in part through improving society as a whole, at least from the perspective of a wide group of elites.

Another major source of motivation was competitive; there was a belief in British society that it could only keep up with such innovative engines as Germany if it solved its social problems. Bentley Gilbert wrote that "[w]hat Germany had that Great Britain did not came to be termed 'national efficiency,'" which was a broad-based term that came to be associated with maximizing human resources: "The quest for national efficiency, therefore, gave social reform what it had not had before—the status of a respectable political question. . . . Only an efficient nation could hold a vigorous, expanding empire."[21] This new conviction was based on the "principle that the physical welfare of the mature working man was a matter of State concern. An efficient nation could not afford to permit its people to suffer the consequences of their own improvidence."[22]

Spurred by those justifications, many groups and individuals played a role in driving reform. At least for a time, a leading source of energy were the Chartists; Chartism was a loose collection of workers and elites focused primarily on political reform and expanding the franchise as the gateway to a broader reform of economic life.[23] Leaders of the movement published

---

and Peter Wende, eds., *Reform in Great Britain and Germany, 1750–1850 (Proceedings of the British Academy)*, Oxford University Press, 1999.

[19] Taylor, 2002, p. 664.

[20] Heffer, 2022, pp. 2–3.

[21] Gilbert, 1966, pp. 60–61.

[22] Gilbert, 1966, p. 101.

[23] Miles Taylor, "Rethinking the Chartists: Searching for Synthesis in the Historiography of Chartism," *Historical Journal*, Vol. 39, No. 2, 1996; Henry Weisser, "Chartism in

the People's Charter in 1838, which included a variety of proposed political reforms—universal male suffrage by secret ballot, salaries for parliament members to allow wider participation, and other steps. The Chartist movement collapsed as a formal organization in the 1850s, but its work had pushed many key issues onto the national stage.

Prince Albert, Queen Victoria's husband, also played an important role in this period as a champion of technological progress and environmental reform, as well as other progressive causes. He lent something of the legitimacy of the Royal family to the trend of reform and renewal and did so in part explicitly inspired by the national competitive value of such reforms. Widely educated and intensely curious, Prince Albert was a patron of the arts, a sponsor and supporter of scientific innovation, an educational reformer, and a believer in the necessity of concern for working classes and governmental modernization.[24]

After the 1840s, highly influential elites—whether politicians, writers, or activists—ranging from Thomas Carlyle to Lord Ashley to Charles Dickens played a critical role in promoting reform.[25] The role of public reports on conditions—even fictional ones—but also analytical investigations, such as the 1861 Newcastle report on elementary education in England, showed stark deficiencies both in the proportion of children attending primary school and the quality of education at that level.[26] It led directly to major legislation on elementary education, the Elementary Education Act of 1870, which transformed the British state's relationship to education.

A major component of the reform effort was voting rights, including those for women. As early as 1832, a Reform Bill had begun to widen the right to vote. The 1867 Reform Act produced a greater increase in enfranchisement and was the culmination of over 15 years' worth of pressure and

---

1848: Reflections on a Non-Revolution," *Albion: A Quarterly Journal Concerned with British Studies*, Vol. 13, No. 1, Spring 1981; Steinbach, 2023, p. 47.

[24] A. N. Wilson, *Prince Albert: The Man Who Saved the Monarchy*, Harper, 2019.

[25] Heffer, 2023, pp. 50–80.

[26] David Ian Allsobrook, *Schools for the Shires: The Reform of Middle-Class Education in Mid-Victorian England*, Manchester University Press, 1986.

debate.[27] A major element of the larger process of social reform was the repeal of the Corn Laws, which boosted agricultural interests by regulating the import and export of grain products. This repeal and other steps gradually weakened the land-holding aristocracy's grip on British life and fueled the rise of a broader middle class. Women's suffrage was a longer battle that gained force in the 1860s but did not produce the first formal extension of the franchise, partial and conditional, until 1918 and was followed by a full extension of voting rights in 1928. However, the groundwork for these movements was laid in the Victorian reform era.[28]

The expanding franchise helped social welfare to become an explicitly political issue. Political parties connected their own fate to policies aimed at the well-being of masses of new working-class voters, which exploded the "implicit agreement" among political parties dominated by elites to ignore the welfare demands of the masses. This was political self-interest in a pure form, rather than any sort of progressive altruism, but it helped make reforms possible.[29]

As social change snowballed, it affected every corner of British life. Some laws, such as the 1833 and 1878 Factory Acts, addressed working conditions in industrial settings. Medical reforms stressed greater professionalism, standardization, and the status of medical professionals in society.[30] Military and civil service reforms pushed for higher standards and merit-based promotion.[31] Other initiatives targeted political corruption through patronage.[32] Education reform took place along many dimensions: There was a simple widening of access, more emphasis on technical and applied fields

---

[27] Robert Saunders, "The Politics of Reform and the Making of the Second Reform Act, 1848–1867," *Historical Journal*, Vol. 50, No. 3, September 2007; Steinbach, 2023, pp. 42–45, 49–53.

[28] Heffer, 2022, pp. 506–573.

[29] Gilbert, 1966, pp. 448–449.

[30] Alison Winter, "Harriet Martineau and the Reform of the Invalid in Victorian England," *Historical Journal*, Vol. 38, No. 3, 1995.

[31] David Fredrick Hood, "The Effects of the Cardwell Reforms on the British Victorian Army," California State University, Fresno, 2001; Heffer, 2022, pp. 469–499.

[32] Philip Harling, *The Waning of "Old Corruption": The Politics of Economical Reform in Britain, 1779–1846*, Clarendon Press, 1996.

(though Britain trailed competing nations in this regard, especially for the aristocratic classes), better treatment of students especially in boarding schools, the broadening of opportunities for young women to be educated, and a breakage of the link between education and the church.[33]

As poverty rose throughout the country, social insurance programs were developed. As hundreds of thousands of impoverished Britons sought aid, the meager public resources devoted to the task—often based in local parishes as provided for by an antiquated Poor Law, which still saw little room for formal government assistance—were exhausted. One of the first responses in the era, the Poor Law of 1834, did not so much as provide assistance but terrify people away from accepting a life of poverty by essentially criminalizing it.[34] It was not until the later Victorian era, or even the early years of the 20th century, that the public assistance matured. Several major pieces of legislation, such as the Education Act and the National Insurance Act, were not passed until 1906 and 1911, respectively.[35] However, they gradually lofted into place a series of remarkable social support systems.

The Results: Dynamism and Influence

It is difficult to track the precise results of this process of reform and modernization in terms of British national power. Clearly, the mid- and late-Victorian era collection of social reforms represent an example of "aristocratic survival by adaptation to changing circumstances."[36] These reforms worked to revitalize British society at a time when an accumulating phalanx of social challenges threatened the legitimacy, dynamism, and stability of the country. As two scholars captured it,

> [t]o outsiders and also to many at home Britain appeared a model community capable of resolving internal conflict without resort to excessive force or revolution. Britain, by the norms of other nations, enjoyed

---

[33] Heffer, 2022, pp. 412–468.

[34] Heffer, 2022, pp. 36–41.

[35] Gilbert, 1966.

[36] Levin, 1998, p. 9.

high degrees of social cohesion and national unity built on consent and co-operation between the governed and the ruling order. This sense of community survived despite the economic difficulties of the period, troubles in Ireland, labour unrest, imperial problems, religious tensions and a hard-fought political contest between competing factions.[37]

The result can be seen in Britain's competitive position in subsequent years. Britain's share of world manufacturing output continued to grow through 1880, reaching a peak of almost 23 percent that year. Even by 1900, British per capita levels of industrialization led the world: Even the United States had only 69 percent of Britain's level by the turn of the 20th century, followed by Germany (at 52 percent of Britain's level), France (at 39 percent), Russia (at 15 percent), and Japan (at 12 percent). By 1890, Britain continued to have the leading gross national product in the world (of $29.4 billion measured in 1960 dollars), though Germany's was catching up (at $26.4 billion) and France's and Russia's were both around $20–$21 billion.[38]

Beyond strictly economic standing, from 1840 through the early 20th century, Britain continued to reflect other measures of societal strength and dynamism. Its political system remained legitimate, its institutions effective, its national identity coherent, and, when challenged, the source of immense resiliency. It remained a significant industrial power even while it was being rapidly bypassed by the United States and Germany.

However, renewal was only temporary. As late as 1938, Britain's per capita industrialization measure was still second in the world, behind a surging United States, only slightly ahead of Germany, and far beyond aspiring modernizers, such as Italy, Russia, and Japan. However, Britain's manufacturing engine was being overtaken in critical sectors. Britain produced only 10.5 million tons of steel in 1938, while Germany produced 23.2 million tons and the United States churned out 28.8 million tons. Even Russia had surpassed Britain in production. In 1938, Britain consumed just 196 million metric tons of coal equivalent in energy; Russia was nearly equal at 177 million tons, Germany had moved ahead at 228 million tons, and the U.S. econ-

---

[37] T. R. Gourvish and Alan O'Day, "Later Victorian Britain," in T. R. Gourvish and Alan O'Day, eds., *Later Victorian Britain, 1867–1900*, Palgrave, 1988.

[38] Kennedy, 1989, pp. 149, 171.

omy consumed an astonishing 697 million-ton equivalents. Britain's relative share of world manufacturing had shrunk from 22.9 percent in 1880 to just 10.7 percent in 1938. Germany now had a larger share (at 12.7 percent), and the United States was the new juggernaut at 31.4 percent.[39]

Britain's slipping position was partly a result of new social, economic, and political challenges, which some observers first identified in the early 20th century but came to true maturity in the 1930s, that have threatened British dynamism for nearly a century and eventually produced what has been described as the "British disease" of stagnating productivity, limited industrial prowess, meager innovation, and institutional malaise. Corelli Barnett was the leading chronicler of the early phases of this process: In *The Collapse of British Power* (1972), he attributed this decline to an idealistic and romantic spirit among the British upper classes, which triumphed over more practical emphases on science and industry, locked the country into the worship of small-scale craftsmen rather than globally competitive major firms, and undermined British dynamism and power. By World War II, he argues, Britain was a secondary industrial and scientific power.[40] Other observers have offered starkly different diagnoses, but whatever the precise causes, Britain has struggled to escape the grip of this long-term stagnation ever since.

---

[39] Kennedy, 1989, pp. 201–202.

[40] Barnett, 1972. See, for example, pp. 27–68, 83–91.

Case Study: Post–Gilded Age United States

The late-19th and early-to-mid-20th century United States offers another leading case of a modern great power rousing itself to avoid an emerging crisis of competitive dynamism. As with the British case, many U.S. officials and reformers of this historical era might be surprised to see their efforts conceived in this way. Perhaps more than in Britain, however, at least some of these advocates of change—especially leaders of the Progressive movement, notably Theodore Roosevelt—were more self-conscious about a larger agenda of change to avert national stagnation or crisis. They were quite explicit in the dangers they identified (though they did not always agree on specific issues) and their connection to national dynamism, as well as the role of their proposed reforms in generating competitive advantage.[1]

Many pieces of this response were unconnected and spontaneous. As in the British case, the overall U.S. process of renewal was as much emergent and unplanned as it was intentional.[2] Even on the core issue of antitrust pol-

---

[1] A classic treatment is Richard Hofstadter, *The Age of Reform: From Bryan to F.D.R.*, Knopf, 1955.

[2] As one scholar notes, "The progressive era seems to be characterized by shifting coalitions around different issues, with the specific nature of these coalitions varying on federal, state and local levels, from region to region, and from the first to the second decades of the century" (Peter G. Filene, "An Obituary for 'The Progressive Movement,'" *American Quarterly*, Vol. 22, No. 1, 1970, p. 33). Another historian argues that "[a]ctually . . . from the 1890's on there were many 'progressive' movements on many levels seeking sometimes contradictory objectives" (Arthur S. Link, "What Happened to the Progressive Movement in the 1920's?" *American Historical Review*, Vol. 64, No. 4, 1959, p. 836).

icies, Theodore Roosevelt disagreed strongly with some more radical members of the movement who wanted to break up big companies as a rule, and, on some issues (notably immigration and racial segregation), the impulses of self-identified Progressives were not always entirely progressive.[3] Still, even in this ad hoc process filled with disagreements, various campaigns, decisions, and trends combined to generate what turned out to be a powerful U.S. agenda for national renewal.

Risks of Decline

The reformers of the Progressive era—and those who picked up elements of their agenda well into the 1960s—were reacting to several leading symptoms of growing national maladies that threatened the competitive position of the United States in the long term.[4] There were significant and sometimes bitter divisions—even among activists calling themselves "Progressive" over basic issues.[5] Perhaps the one theme that most commonly united this diverse and often contentious collection of groups and activists was a concern for the growing dominance of monopolistic big business over U.S. life, as well as the resulting economic inequality and perceived threat to the future of democracy. These groups and activists were responding to objective trends in wealth and income: By 1890, the wealthiest 1 percent of

---

[3] One especially skeptical treatment of the movement is Michael E. McGerr, *A Fierce Discontent: The Rise and Fall of the Progressive Movement in America, 1870–1920*, Free Press, 2003.

[4] For general treatments of the movement, see John Whiteclay Chambers II, *The Tyranny of Change: America in the Progressive Era, 1890–1920*, 2nd ed., Rutgers University Press, 2000; James T. Kloppenberg, *Uncertain Victory: Social Democracy and Progressivism in European and American Thought, 1870–1920*, Oxford University Press, 1986; and Daniel T. Rodgers, *Atlantic Crossings: Social Politics in a Progressive Age*, Harvard University Press, 2000.

[5] "Progressives could be found who admired the efficiency of the big corporation and who detested the trusts, who lauded the 'people' and who yearned for an electorate confined to white and educated voters, who spoke the language of social engineering and the language of moralistic uplift, or (to make matters worse) did all these things at once" (Daniel T. Rodgers, "In Search of Progressivism," *Reviews in American History*, Vol. 10, No. 4, 1982, p. 122).

Americans owned an estimated 51 percent of property; the 40 percent of Americans at the bottom of the wealth ladder owned just 1.2 percent. The top 12 percent of the richest families controlled almost 90 percent of the nation's wealth.[6]

Progressives also railed against corruption in U.S. politics at the time, including tight links between politicians and major corporate interests. They saw the rise of political machines at various levels, from municipal to national, as a long-term threat to democracy and demanded various political reforms, including early versions of campaign finance regulations, to control the influence of private interests over public policy. Some Progressives—but by no means all—worried about the constraints on group opportunity that plagued the United States at this time: The movement contained an odd mixture of socioeconomic radicalism and, in some cases, support for segregation and racial bias.

More broadly, Progressive reformers worried about the threat to long-term national dynamism from uncontrolled industrialization. As in Britain, rapid and largely unmodulated industrial development in the United States was producing increasingly unlivable cities, often abusive factory jobs, and environmental disasters. The result was a growing corrosion in the legitimacy of the national model and significant measurable effects on national energy and cohesion. Progressive reformers favored legislation to regulate the activities of corporations. Many Progressives were concerned in parallel terms with rising inequality and a growing concentration of wealth, which some believed could undermine national cohesion in ways that threatened U.S. competitive strength. Progressives had a "yearning for rebirth" and sought to inject "some visceral vitality into a modern culture that had seemed brittle and about to collapse."[7]

---

[6] Nell Irvin Painter, *Standing at Armageddon: A Grassroots History of the Progressive Era*, W. W. Norton, 2008, pp. 8, 16.

[7] Jackson Lears, *Rebirth of a Nation: The Making of Modern America, 1877–1920*, HarperPerennial, 2010, pp. 8, 9.

The Agenda of Reform

In response to these maladies, reformers pushed on many fronts and often disagreed about key policies. Even the issue of women's suffrage did not garner universal support from self-identified Progressives.[8] But Progressives and other advocates for change managed to generate movement on many mutually supporting issues, from shared opportunity to an active state. The result was a country that was strengthened and more resilient in ways that underpinned its competitive position for over half a century and set the stage for the peak of U.S. national dynamism between roughly 1940 and 1970.

In the process, this U.S. response, which was parallel to Britain's renewal during the Victorian era, ended up addressing each of the seven characteristics of national competitive advantage outlined in the first phase of this study and identified as critical to many cases of peak national power. The result was the sort of helpful feedback loop among these characteristics. It was not a direct trajectory: Between 1890 and 1929, wealth inequality and other measures of national renewal "oscillated wildly" and did not reflect a simple trend.[9] But the general movement of legislation and shared public thinking on social issues in these decades shifted in ways that helped address increasing dangers with enduring success. In part, the general movement did so because the resulting consensus came to guide major elements of both major political parties.

The reformers undertook many steps to enhance opportunities and increase equality—in both its objective measures and its perception. These included expanding suffrage and generating commitments that led to broader empowerment in ways that were not necessarily intended by some Progressive reformers who were less committed to racial equality. Progressives supported breaking up corporate monopolies, though to different degrees and with different strategies. Many supported protections for unions and laws protecting labor, as well as anti-corruption policies, such as the direct election of senators and early campaign-finance laws.

---

[8] Filene (1970) outlines the many disagreements within the movement.

[9] Robert D. Putnam, *The Upswing: How America Came Together a Century Ago and How We Can Do It Again*, Simon and Schuster, 2022, pp. 38–39.

The result was a flurry of laws that changed the government's role in promoting national stability and dynamism. These laws included the 1906 Pure Food and Drug Act (which created the Food and Drug Administration), workplace safety laws, the Sherman and Clayton Antitrust Acts, the establishment of the National Park Service and National Forest Service and creation of many national parks, the Federal Reserve Act of 1913, various child labor laws, the 17th Amendment to the Constitution mandating direct election of senators, the 19th Amendment guaranteeing women's suffrage, and laws regarding workers' compensation and a graduated income tax.[10]

The trends in public attitudes regarding such issues after 1870 were of equal importance in setting the stage for continued public policies to underwrite national coherence and dynamism. As one historian explains,

> [t]he New Deal could proceed without a Wilson, a Croly, or a Brandeis, because such men had already done their work. The task of criticizing the old ideas and shaping the new had largely been completed *during the Progressive Era*. It was because the basic thinking had already been done that the general approach to the crisis, as distinct from particular programs, could be agreed upon so quickly and with so little need for agonizing reappraisal.[11]

This is a major theme of Robert Putnam's assessment of the U.S. rise to competitive dominance before and after World War II: The reformist sentiments of the late 19th century built a foundation of shared beliefs about desired national outcomes that continued to inspire and underwrite reforms right through the 1960s. Putnam argued that "Progressive Era social innovations and institutional reforms put the US on a new path toward greater economic equality, laying the foundations" for what he called "the Great Convergence" of incomes and opportunity "that lasted until the 1970s. Progressive Era reformers . . . created innovations such as the public high school, labor unions, the federal tax structure, antitrust

---

[10] Painter, 2008, p. 36.

[11] Andrew M. Scott, "The Progressive Era in Perspective," *Journal of Politics*, Vol. 21, No. 4, 1959, p. 697. Painter (2008, p. 515) agrees that the New Deal was the "culmination of Progressive Era politics," which sought "to make government the protector of ordinary people."

legislation, financial regulation, and more." They were, he contends, "the necessary foundations for further developments . . . that underpinned the Great Convergence."[12]

The Results: Dynamism and Influence

The reasons for the relative success of the Progressive movement—as an example of coalition politics rather than as a coherent and singular movement—remain contested. One argument is somewhat paradoxical: The various interest groups that pushed for change came to the fore at a time when voting was in decline and parties were weakened, which would have seemed to signal a moment of political inactivity but opened the door to groups that may have been shut out of politics before.[13] Some historians see the Progressive era as a signal of looming changes in U.S. politics, such as issue-specific movements and professionalized activism.

Nor did the era involve a straight-line trajectory toward the solution of social ills or to national renewal. Terrible recessions occurred in the 1870s and 1890s; in the latter years, up to one-third of the workforce was unemployed in some states, which helped generate significant social unrest, including labor strikes, marches of tramp or laborer "armies" in Washington, D.C., and race riots. The 1920s saw a renewed Gilded Age, one that might have pushed the country away from the reform mindset of the late 19th century had it not been for the Great Depression. The 1920s was a time

> when the political representatives of big business and Wall Street executed a relentless and successful campaign in state and nation to subvert the regulatory structure that had been built at the cost of so much toil and sweat since the 1870's, and to restore a Hanna-like reign of special privilege to benefit business, industry, and finance.[14]

---

[12] Putnam, 2022, p. 46.

[13] Rodgers, 1982, pp. 115–116.

[14] Link, 1959, p. 834.

The pace of reform measures rose and fell during these decades depending on conditions: During bursts of prosperity, the incentive for reforms tended to dampen amid a general "temptation to leave well enough alone" when economic trends seemed positive.[15]

A growing, muckraking press played a critical role in encouraging change. It attacked political corruption and lampooned oligarchs, publicized awful working conditions, called for bold economic change, and promoted the populist and Progressive cause in the larger population in other ways.[16] Independent commissions played a significant role as well in documenting labor, environmental, and living conditions that demanded change.

Nonetheless, the many reform measures that were introduced from the 1870s through the 1910s changed U.S. society. Key legislation and activism— on antitrust, labor rights and union organizing, campaign finance, and women's suffrage—shifted the balance of power between workers and big business on the one hand and voters and political parties on the other. Debates began almost immediately about the significance and persistence of these changes; many historians have argued that the Progressive movement hardly dented big business' influence, and some even view the movement as conveying the impression of change where little had actually occurred. Nevertheless, there were significant changes to legislation and, especially, the expectations about the role of government that helped to set the stage for national renewal.

One result was measurable changes in key gauges of social equality and justice, which are harder to track in these earlier periods in which data are scarce (and are generally believed to have backslid in the 1920s). However, the eventual result of changes sparked in the 1870s was a different United States. As noted above, these changes cascaded and laid the groundwork for more measurable improvements in equity in later decades. In the three decades after World War II, for example, "the post-tax and transfer income of the poorest 20 percent grew three times faster than the income of the

---

[15] Painter, 2008, pp. 48, 179; the quoted text is from p. 251.

[16] Painter, 2008, pp. 258, 271–277.

richest 1 percent." Intergenerational mobility rose to a modern peak: More than 90 percent of U.S. children earned more than their parents.[17]

The United States' impressive response to a compelling set of risks from the end of the 19th century through the mid-20th century reaffirms one conclusion of this report's companion paper, about the ways that nations align themselves to the competitive paradigm of an era. That paper suggests that meeting the demands of an era requires two essential things: (1) mastering the model of value creation of the era and (2) developing an effective and updated social contract to generate legitimacy for the society and its governing structures.[18] In addition to addressing elements of all seven characteristics of national competitive advantage, the U.S. agenda of reform and response in this period also helped the United States to meet these two critical requirements of competitive advantage. Several of the forms of response noted above, such as government investment in research and development, catalyzed new industries that helped the country master the evolving models of value creation. And the multiple steps to reinvigorate the country's sociopolitical model infused it with a fresh legitimacy by updating and modernizing the nation's social contract.

The era reflected something less measurable than economic statistics or the roster of specific reforms: It embodied, as Jackson Lears put it, a "widespread yearning for regeneration—for rebirth that was variously spiritual, moral, and physical—[that] penetrated public life, inspiring movements and policies that formed the foundation for U.S. society in the twentieth century."[19] Such an intense urge for national expression could have easily trended toward overreach abroad, producing nationalistic ambitions and foreign adventures. However, an important lesson for the question of national renewal is the importance of the right national spirit or mindset—a general commitment to rebirth. As another historian put it, "To survive, a democracy must be able to recognize important social needs and meet them before they generate explosive forces. The broad question confronting the Progressive Era was whether American democracy could meet the challenge

---

[17] Putnam, 2022, pp. 39, 41.

[18] Mazarr, Dale-Huang, and Sargent, 2024.

[19] Lears, 2010, p. 1.

that had arisen."[20] The reformist surge beginning in the 1870s sought to respond with nothing less than a "rethinking and reconstruction of American life."[21]

---

[20] Scott, 1959, p. 699.

[21] Scott, 1959, p. 701.

Case Study: Late–Cold War Soviet Union

Our third case reflects a failed effort at renewal—the Soviet Union's drive for reform in the mid- to late-1980s. In this case, national leaders were intensely aware of the reality of an intensifying crisis and the risk of rapid decline. Soviet leaders from Yuri Andropov onward tried to take steps to renew their system. These failed efforts offer lessons for the broader issue of national renewal.

Risks of Decline

Like Britain and the United States, the Soviet Union had achieved a leading position among the great powers only to see its position imperiled by social, economic, and political challenges. From the 1920s through the 1950s, the USSR generated significant economic results, which led Soviet leaders to believe that it would overtake the West economically and technologically, through much of the 1960s.[1] Nikita Khrushchev predicted in 1957 that the USSR would "catch up and surpass America"; later, he promised that the next generation of Soviet citizens would live in a communist paradise.[2] This optimism partly resulted from the intellectual opening that came with de-Stalinization starting in 1956, as well as the sense of restraints being released

---

[1] Chris Miller, *The Struggle to Save the Soviet Economy: Mikhail Gorbachev and the Collapse of the USSR*, University of North Carolina Press, 2016, p. 17.

[2] Vladislav M. Zubok, *A Failed Empire: The Soviet Union in the Cold War from Stalin to Gorbachev*, University of North Carolina Press, 2007, p. 175.

and a new possibility of open dialogue and investigation.[3] This was an era of fervent patriotism in the USSR and the rise of "enlightened" apparatchiks, technocrats, and scientists who saw a more humane and effective possibility for the Soviet future. As Khrushchev's son-in-law said of this era, "We had no feeling of failure, deadlock or stagnation. I would like to stress: there was still the reserve of energy, many remained optimistic."[4]

Moscow's main rival—the United States—seemed in real crisis from the late 1960s through the late 1970s. Social strife around Vietnam and civil rights was burgeoning. The oil crisis of the 1970s mauled the U.S. economy, which shrank by 6 percent between 1973 and 1975; meanwhile, the late 1960s saw discoveries of massive new oil fields in the USSR, which were coming to generate 80 percent of Soviet foreign exchange earnings. Soviet observers could be forgiven for thinking that some of the forecasts of Marxist-Leninist dogma were unfolding before their eyes.[5] Even by 1985, however, "the Soviet economy was wasteful and poorly managed, but it was not in crisis."[6] As Stephen Kotkin put it, the USSR was "lethargically stable and could have continued muddling on for quite some time."[7]

Yet the need for change had become obvious by the late 1970s, if only to have any hope of keeping up with the United States. As early as the late 1950s, there was a widespread appreciation for the "rigid bureaucratic apparatus that held the country in steel bands and blocked innovation and change,"[8] as Vladislav Zubok put it. Soviet leaders were never able to escape the constant, crushing comparison with the West; any Russian citizens who took advantage of the more open environment to travel in Europe or Asia came back with a clear impression of how quickly the industrialized world was moving. At the same time, the opening prodded the embers of regional

[3] Zubok, 2007, pp. 166, 175–177.

[4] Zubok, 2007, p. 178.

[5] Stephen Kotkin, *Armageddon Averted: The Soviet Collapse, 1970–2000*, Oxford University Press, 2001, pp. 29–33.

[6] Miller, 2016, p. 60.

[7] Kotkin, 2001, p. 2.

[8] Zubok, 2007, p. 179.

nationalism and ethnic identity to life, stoking the force that would ultimately fracture Moscow's force-bound multiethnic empire.

By the late 1960s, several developments hammered home the limits of reform and the persistent stagnation of the Soviet system. Growing public disaffection led Khrushchev himself to turn against the liberalizing technocrats, cracking down on public dissent and bringing a sharp end to the hope for a more open future. Zubok noted that "the utopian energies that nourished Soviet patriotism had been exhausted. Soviet identity, rejuvenated by these energies, also began to fragment and erode under powerful external and internal influences."[9] The result of the 1956–1968 period was a failed lunge at partial reform, which "ended up alienating the cultural, intellectual, and scientific elites that had been the most optimistic and patriotic at the beginning of the 'great' decade."[10] By the era of Leonid Brezhnev, any real hope of serious reform was shelved, and the Soviet government "was content to live with the fossilized ideology and sought to repress cultural dissent and force its participants into exile and immigration."[11] The era spawned a period of orthodox officials who lacked imagination and sought mainly to keep the gears turning—however roughly and inefficiently.

A new generation of officials with reformist tendencies, such as Gorbachev, recognized the lack of energy in the system by this time. Gorbachev had begun to travel to the West and was struck by the better standard of living in the capitalist countries. By 1975, Gorbachev had become both concerned and bold enough to confront Andropov directly about whether he and other senior leaders "were really thinking about the good of the country."[12]

The decline accelerated in the late Brezhnev, Andropov, and Konstantin Chernenko years (1978–1985). Within and outside the Soviet Union, the degree of economic decline and loosening legitimacy in Eastern Europe was known but not fully appreciated. By 1980, when labor strikes and then wide-

---

[9] Zubok, 2007, p. 191.

[10] Zubok, 2007, p. 191.

[11] Zubok, 2007, p. 191.

[12] William Taubman, *Gorbachev: His Life and Times*, Simon and Schuster, 2017, pp. 116–117, 139.

spread protests erupted in Poland, the Politburo decided it simply could not afford to intervene. Moscow had come to at least partly recognize that its global posture was bankrupting it: By that time, the Soviet Union was propping up 69 satellite and client states and spending one-quarter of its GDP on military power.[13] Sanctions imposed after December 1979, including on U.S. grain and high technology embargoes, further hurt Soviet economic and technological potential, as did the impact on Soviet legitimacy.[14] Soviet growth was stagnating, birth rates were falling, life expectancy was declining, consumer goods were often in shortage, and the quality of those goods was often terrible.

By the time Gorbachev became General Secretary, the Soviet system was clearly headed for trouble. Many analyses made clear that it was lagging badly in productivity, output, and overall dynamism compared with the West.[15] The need for bolder reform was clear to anyone looking at the evidence; as Kotkin puts it, major trends suggested that "the competition with capitalism—not a policy but something inherent to the system's identity and survival—was unwinnable."[16] The problem was that there was no obvious way to achieve the necessary changes without totally disrupting a system built to ensure stasis.

The Agenda of Reform

Soviet leaders including Gorbachev remained true believers in their socialist system and were convinced that it could be reenergized through the right reforms, which would create a socialist market system with new dynamism and competitive potential. They were inspired in part by the Chinese case, in which Deng Xiaoping's reforms were already generating significant growth, and by some Eastern European countries, in which limited reforms

---

[13] Zubok, 2007, pp. 266–268.

[14] Rafael Reuveny and Aseem Prakash, "The Afghanistan War and the Breakdown of the Soviet Union," *Review of International Studies*, Vol. 25, 1999.

[15] Abram Bergson, "Comparative Productivity: The USSR, Eastern Europe, and the West," *American Economic Review*, Vol. 77, No. 3, 1987.

[16] Kotkin, 2001, p. 26.

had been tried in communist systems. Soviet analysts also looked to Japan as an industrial power that relied on stronger state intervention than the United States and was, by the 1980s, seemingly poised to overtake a crisis-prone and industrially hollowed United States. Even critics supported many aspects of Perestroika in the early years, in part because they recognized that change was essential.[17]

Gorbachev's reform plan had two immense handicaps from the beginning. First, it was a top-down series of directives that never managed to unleash the sort of pluralistic collection of problem-solving mechanisms that arose in the British and U.S. cases. Second, Gorbachev knew what he wanted to do—he just "had no idea how" to actually renew the Soviet model.[18] He would improvise, prevaricate, and experiment, but he never settled on a truly coherent reform strategy, all the while sidestepping many of the changes needed for a real revitalization. He was constrained by political boundaries, especially at the beginning, which hemmed in his efforts for the first two years.[19]

What Gorbachev eventually hit on was a somewhat ad hoc collection of steps that looked fairly conventional from the standpoint of pump-priming communist systems. He tried an anti-corruption drive, which was already emphasized under Andropov's leadership, with the hope of improving the quality of officials, the efficiency of state activity, and work discipline. He sought to boost investment in heavy industry with the ambition of boosting production by over 20 percent. He aimed to match U.S. industrial production levels by 2000.[20] To create a permissive environment for this vision, Gorbachev began to undertake international initiatives to produce a super-charged version of détente that would provide a permissive environment for his domestic revitalization plans. As William Taubman related, years later Gorbachev claimed that his original plan was to "combine socialism with

---

[17] Miller, 2016, pp. 2–3, 12, 19–25.

[18] Boettke argues that the central problem was that Gorbachev never truly implemented any one reform element in his agenda. See Peter Boettke, *Why Perestroika Failed: The Politics and Economics of Socialist Transformation*, Palgrave, 1993. See also Zubok, 2007, p. 279.

[19] Taubman, 2017, pp. 213–215.

[20] Taubman, 2017, pp. 217, 237–237; Zubok, 2007, p. 279.

the scientific and technological revolution"; however, "[t]hat wasn't a plan. It was a hope."[21]

This was all moving at a gradual pace until April 1986 when the Chernobyl disaster struck, constituting the biggest single blow to the credibility of the Soviet system yet. It revealed that the inefficiency and corruption of the Soviet bureaucracy and destroyed Soviet legitimacy in the eyes of the world.[22] "Chernobyl's effect on the Soviet political leadership," Zubok wrote, "was greater than any other single event since the Cuban missile crisis."[23]

Even by the late 1980s, the content of Gorbachev's reform program remained unclear and shifting; it was unable to resolve essential dilemmas of control versus openness, state-led industrialization versus private initiative. His posture was a diagnosis without a cure. By this time, the Soviet system had likely suppressed any possibility for independent initiative rendering regeneration impossible.

Falling oil prices exacerbated the Soviet Union's crisis in the mid-1980s. Oil had risen steadily in price during the 1970s, which provided a critical source of hard currency for Moscow and helped successive regimes camouflage the decay of the system. However, the profits were thrown into foreign adventures, food imports to make up for domestic shortfalls, or subsidizing inefficient industries; when the price of oil collapsed in 1986 from about $30 a barrel to $12–$15, it had a huge impact on Soviet state finances.[24] A 1986 report from the U.S. Central Intelligence Agency estimated that the collapse in Russian earnings would cut its imports by as much as one-third "at a time when Gorbachev is probably counting on increased inputs from the

---

[21] Taubman, 2017, p. 219.

[22] The classic treatment of this issue is Serhii Plokhy, *Chernobyl: The History of a Nuclear Catastrophe*, Basic Books, 2020. See also Serhii Plokhy, "Chernobyl and the Fall of the Soviet Union," University of New South Wales, Centre for Ideas, undated.

[23] Zubok, 2017, p. 288.

[24] Michael Dobbs, "Oil's Skid Fuels Gorbachev's Reforms," *Washington Post*, May 28, 1990; Douglas B. Reynolds, "Soviet Economic Decline: Did an Oil Crisis Cause the Transition in the Soviet Union?" *Journal of Energy and Development*, Vol. 24, No. 1, 1998.

West to assist his program of economic revitalization."[25] The decline in oil prices was only one of several factors emptying out Soviet coffers, but it was a significant one.[26] The oil crisis also reaffirmed problems with innovation: Soviet oil firms did not have the technology to keep supplies flowing.

By 1987, Gorbachev had embraced the need for much deeper economic and political reform, but it was still not clear what this reform would be. He had "moved on to ideas of radically transforming Soviet ideology and the political and economic systems and truly opening the Soviet Union to the world."[27] Ultimately, Gorbachev would still hesitate on the most important changes, such as price adjustments. He tried to recruit support for change from outside the Communist party and, in the process, accelerated the party's loss of legitimacy.

The Results: Failed Reforms, Stunted Renewal

Gorbachev's reforms achieved the opposite of what he intended: They destroyed, rather than renewed, the Soviet Union.[28] He would not risk public disapproval with steps such as price reform. He rallied support from fresh social forces outside the regime rather than connecting over common cause with fellow reformers inside it. He began to pull apart the Soviet system before knowing what the new model would look like. In sum, "Gorbachev's 'remedies' were killing the sick patient."[29] His push into truly radical domestic steps after 1987 "created a most severe crisis of the state and produced

---

[25] U.S. Central Intelligence Agency, Office of Soviet Analysis, "USSR: Facing the Dilemma of Hard Currency Shortages," SOV 86-10027 X, May 1986, sanitized copy released December 1, 2011, p. iii.

[26] Kotkin, 2001, p. 33.

[27] Zubok, 2007, p. 302. See also Anders Åslund, *Gorbachev's Struggle for Economic Reform: The Soviet Reform Process, 1985–1988*, Cornell University Press, 1989.

[28] This is the major argument of Kotkin (2001). See also Mark Harrison, "Coercion, Compliance, and the Collapse of the Soviet Command Economy," *Economic History Review*, Vol. 55, No. 3, August 2002.

[29] Zubok, 2007, p. 307.

centrifugal political forces that spun out of control within Soviet society."[30] One lesson, Zubok concludes, is that "[r]eform has to have support of a criti-cal mass of elites, not just radical intellectuals who will be impelled to turn on reformists in favor of demands for radical change."[31]

Zubok argues that "it is possible to imagine a gradual transformation of the post-Stalinist Communist model into a post-Communist authoritar-ian model (as has been taking place in China). A leader supported by the pragmatic elements of the top party circles might have gradually privatized state property."[32] Chris Miller agrees that the Soviet Union of the mid-1980s still enjoyed several advantages: Strong global markets for its minerals, a sophisticated scientific sector that had produced important technological advances, and an educated population. "It was not wholly unrealistic to think—as did Gorbachev and many of his advisors—that with a bit more flexibility and extra funding for new technology, the USSR could be a major beneficiary of the computer age rather than its most prominent victim." The Soviet system had, after all, demonstrated "a remarkable ability to preserve itself."[33] Many accounts suggest that, with some clever tweaking around the edges, Soviet leaders could have kept the system grinding for-ward for decades.

As Gorbachev and others realized, however, the USSR had clearly entered a spiral of decay and lost legitimacy. It was already proving inca-pable of keeping up with the United States in the emerging information age. After moments of hope in the 1970s that capitalism was entering a crisis, within just a decade it became clear to Soviet leaders that longer-term trends in dynamism, innovation, and legitimacy had turned decisively against them. The question, again, was what to do about it and whether any agenda of reform existed that could make the Soviet model competitive without attacking its core nature.

The impossible dilemmas involved in reforming the Soviet system were readily apparent in one of Gorbachev's early initiatives—an anti-alcohol

---

[30] Zubok, 2007, p. 307.

[31] Zubok, 2007, p. 308.

[32] Zubok, 2007, p. 308.

[33] Miller, 2016, p. 147. See also Kotkin, 2001, p. 42.

drive designed to address the immense economic costs of rampant alcoholism throughout Russian society. Gorbachev boosted taxes on alcoholic beverages and banned its sale during certain hours. Consumption did decline—and with it, state revenues from its sale. Soviet officials later claimed that before the campaign, Soviet citizens bought 54 billion rubles worth of alcohol, 16 percent of all retail sales in the USSR. After the crackdown, the total plummeted to 11 billion rubles. This difference equaled the lost revenue from declining world oil prices.[34] Gorbachev could not create a modern economy with a country full of alcoholics, but, in attacking that problem, he undermined the financial basis for his ideas.

At the core of the failure was the role of key Soviet elites and interest groups (the historian Chris Miller identifies these groups as the military, agricultural interests, and the energy industry), which would not agree to significant cuts in their budgets and had the power to obstruct any General Secretary who tried to make such cuts. These sectors soaked up a huge proportion of Soviet budgets and efforts: According to a 1989 estimate, the defense industry alone was responsible for three-quarters of the scientific research in the country and 60 percent of its steel use.[35] However, these sectors were fenced off from major reforms because of their political power. Meanwhile, despite the general appreciation of a need for reform, broader networks of elites opposed reforms that would undermine their privileges.[36]

The Soviet system also created space for literally thousands of governing entities—from specific firms to local governments—to take self-serving actions that undermined the general direction of reform; as central control waned, the system fragmented into one made up of hundreds of lower-level points of decision. Part of the challenge was the legacy of the post-Stalinist reforms: As the Soviet system eased off of a totalitarian level of central control, space was opened for major interests in the economy to engage in self-

---

[34] Miller, 2016, p. 62.

[35] Miller, 2016, pp. 4, 55–72, 178–183.

[36] Vladislav M. Zubok, "The Collapse of the Soviet Union: Leadership, Elites, and Legitimacy," in Geir Lundestad, ed., *The Fall of Great Powers: Peace, Stability, and Legitimacy*, Oxford University Press, 1994, pp. 161–165.

directed bargaining and manipulation; over time, this process of bureaucratic and institutional self-promotion became firmly entrenched.[37]

Meanwhile, the price of subsidizing consumer prices was immense (the state paid for one-third of every loaf of bread, half the cost of milk, and almost three-quarters of the cost of beef[38]), and it continued to distort incentives within the system in ways that crippled reforms. Yet Gorbachev could not bring himself to slash the subsidies because he feared a massive political backlash.

These tensions resulted in a burgeoning financial crisis. The Kremlin was losing income because of falling oil prices, declining liquor revenues, and other gaps, yet it could not cut subsidies or state support to key industries. It responded initially by simply printing money, which spurred inflation. Gorbachev appears to have been hoping that he could prompt enough new economic activity to grow his way out of these dilemmas, but almost no amount of economic growth would have done that. By the late 1980s, Moscow was running deficits equal to 10 percent of GDP; in 1991, it peaked at three times that percentage.[39]

All the while, Gorbachev and other reformers had to deal with what was perhaps the leading dilemma: The Communist party was the only entity in the USSR capable of forcing through needed changes, but chipping away at the party's authority was a necessary component of any major reforms. This irresolvable contradiction led Gorbachev finally to seek support outside the party through a wider array of socioeconomic actors, but in so doing, he radicalized the most conservative opponents against him.[40] William Taubman explained that the trouble was

> [t]hat [the Soviet system] relied on what had caused the economic stagnation in the first place. The rigid central planning process, along

---

[37] Hanson argues that this process was central to the story of Soviet economic decline. See Philip Hanson, *The Rise and Fall of the Soviet Economy*, Longman, 2003.

[38] Miller, 2016, p. 66.

[39] Miller, 2016, p. 145.

[40] Alec Nove, "The Fall of Empires—Russia and the Soviet Union," in Geir Lundestad, ed., *The Fall of Great Powers: Peace, Stability, and Legitimacy*, Oxford University Press, 1994, p. 141. See also Kotkin, 2001, p. 97.

with pervasive secrecy, stifled scientific and technical innovation. The machine-building enterprises Gorbachev wanted to encourage struggled to find customers for their low-quality production. Agricultural output lagged even as state subsidies designed to boost it ballooned.[41]

Stephen Kotkin refers to the "recurring contradictions in the Sisyphean attempts to have the planned economy reform itself, without undoing planning or socialism."[42] The reform drive made clear "that the revolution's ideals were embedded in institutions that made them not only unrealized but also unrealizable."[43] The reform itself took a teetering socioeconomic system and pushed it off a cliff edge, leading to an economic collapse in the early 1990s that discredited the system far more fully than it had been by any other prior events.

---

[41] Taubman, 2017, p. 238.

[42] Kotkin, 2001, p. 65.

[43] Kotkin, 2001, p. 176.

References

Alatas, Syed Farid, "Luxury, State and Society: The Theme of Enslavement in Ibn Khaldûn," *Journal of Historical Sociology*, Vol. 30, No. 1, March 2017.

Albertson, Kevin, and Paul Stepney, "1979 and All That: A 40-Year Reassessment of Margaret Thatcher's Legacy on Her Own Terms," *Cambridge Journal of Economics*, Vol. 44, No. 2, March 2020.

Allsobrook, David Ian, *Schools for the Shires: The Reform of Middle-Class Education in Mid-Victorian England*, Manchester University Press, 1986.

Álvarez-Nogal, Carlos, and Leandro Prados De La Escosura, "The Rise and Fall of Spain (1270–1850)," *Economic History Review*, Vol. 66, No. 1, February 2013.

Åslund, Anders, *Gorbachev's Struggle for Economic Reform: The Soviet Reform Process, 1985–1988*, Cornell University Press, 1989.

Baccaro, Lucio, and Chris Howell, *Trajectories of Neoliberal Transformation: European Industrial Relations Since the 1970s*, Cambridge University Press, 2017.

Barnett, Correlli, *The Collapse of British Power*, Eyre Methuen, 1972.

Barsky, Robert B., and Luts Kilian, *A Monetary Explanation of the Great Stagflation of the 1970s*, National Bureau of Economic Research, Working Paper No. 7547, February 2000.

Bergson, Abram, "Comparative Productivity: The USSR, Eastern Europe, and the West," *American Economic Review*, Vol. 77, No. 3, 1987.

Blanning, T. C. W., and Peter Wende, eds., *Reform in Great Britain and Germany 1750–1850 (Proceedings of the British Academy)*, Oxford University Press, 1999.

Boettke, Peter J., *Why Perestroika Failed: The Politics and Economics of Socialist Transformation*, Palgrave, 1993.

Bouscasse, Paul, Emi Nakamura, and Jón Steinsson, "When Did Growth Begin? New Estimates of Productivity Growth in England from 1250 to 1870," National Bureau of Economic Research, Working Paper 28623, revised March 2023.

Bozeman, Adda B., "Decline of the West? Spengler Reconsidered," *Virginia Quarterly Review*, Spring 1983.

Broadberry, Stephen, Bruce M.S S. Campbell, Alexander Klein, Mark Overton, and Bas van Leeuwen, "Britain in an International Context," in *British Economic Growth, 1270–1870*, Cambridge University Press, 2015.

Brundage, Anthony, "Reform of the Poor Law Electoral System, 1834–94," *Albion: A Quarterly Journal Concerned with British Studies*, Vol. 7, No. 3, 1975.

Centeno, Miguel A., Peter W. Callahan, Paul A. Larcey, and Thayer S. Patterson, "Globalization and Fragility: A Systems Approach to Collapse," in Miguel A. Centeno, Peter W. Callahan, Paul A. Larcey, and Thayer S. Patterson, eds., *How Worlds Collapse: What History, Systems, and Complexity Can Teach About Our Modern World and Fragile Future*, Routledge, 2023.

Chambers, John Whiteclay, II, *The Tyranny of Change: America in the Progressive Era, 1890–1920*, 2nd ed., Rutgers University Press, 2000.

Crafts, Nicholas, and Terence C. Mills, "Is the UK Productivity Slowdown Unprecedented?" *National Institute Economic Review*, Vol. 251, February 2020.

David, Miriam E., "What Were the Lasting Effects of Thatcher's Legacy for Families in the UK?" in Stephen Farrall and Colin Hay, eds., *The Legacy of Thatcherism: Assessing and Exploring Thatcherite Social and Economic Policies*, British Academy Original Paperbacks, 2014.

de Vries, Jan, and Ad Van Der Woude, *The First Modern Economy: Success, Failure, and Perseverance of the Dutch Economy, 1500–1815*, Cambridge University, 1997.

Diamond, Jared, *Collapse: How Societies Choose to Succeed or Fail*, Viking Penguin, 2005.

Dobbs, Michael, "Oil's Skid Fuels Gorbachev's Reforms," *Washington Post*, May 28, 1990.

Drake, William J., and Kalypso Nicolaidis, "Ideas, Interests, and Institutionalism: 'Trade in Services' and the Uruguay Round," *International Organization*, Vol. 46, No. 1, 1992.

Espiet-Kilty, Raphaële, "The Legacy of Thatcherism in Question: An Introduction," *Observatoire de la société britannique*, Vol. 17, 2015.

Faulseit, Ronald K., *Beyond Collapse: Archaeological Perspectives on Resilience, Revitalization, and Transformation in Complex Societies*, Southern Illinois University Press, 2016.

Ferguson, Niall, *Doom: The Politics of Catastrophe*, Penguin, 2021.

Filene, Peter G., "An Obituary for 'The Progressive Movement,'" *American Quarterly*, Vol. 22, No. 1, 1970.

Friedberg, Aaron L., *The Weary Titan: Britain and the Experience of Relative Decline, 1895–1905*, Princeton University Press, 2010.

Gaddis, John Lewis, *The Landscape of History: How Historians Map the Past*, Oxford University Press, 2004.

Gamble, Andrew, *Britain in Decline: Economic Policy, Political Strategy and the British State*, St. Martin's Press, 1994.

Gibbon, Edward, *The History of the Decline and Fall of the Roman Empire*, Strahan & Cadell, originally published 1776–1789.

Gilbert, Bentley B., *The Evolution of National Insurance in Great Britain: The Origins of the Welfare State*, Michael Joseph, 1966.

Gilpin, Robert, *War and Change in International Politics*, Cambridge University Press, 1981.

Goldstone, Jack A., *Revolution and Rebellion in the Early Modern World*, University of California Press, 1991.

Goldstone, Jack A., "Efflorescences and Economic Growth in World History: Rethinking the 'Rise of the West' and the Industrial Revolution," *Journal of World History*, Vol. 13, No. 2, Fall 2002.

Gough, Clair, and Simon Shackley, "The Respectable Politics of Climate Change: The Epistemic Communities and NGOs," *International Affairs*, Vol. 77, No. 2, April 2001.

Gourvish, T. R., and Alan O'Day, "Later Victorian Britain," in T. R. Gourvish and Alan O'Day, eds., *Later Victorian Britain, 1867–1900*, Palgrave, 1988.

Haas, Peter M., "Policy Knowledge: Epistemic Communities," in Neil J. Smelser and Paul B. Baltes, eds., *International Encyclopedia of Social and Behavioral Sciences*, Pergamon, 2001.

Haggard, Robert F., *The Persistence of Victorian Liberalism: The Politics of Social Reform in Britain, 1870–1900*, Greenwood Press, 2001.

Hanson, Philip, *The Rise and Fall of the Soviet Economy*, Longman, 2003.

Harling, Philip, *The Waning of "Old Corruption": The Politics of Economical Reform in Britain, 1779–1846*, Clarendon Press, 1996.

Harrison, Lawrence E., and Samuel P. Huntington, eds., *Culture Matters: How Values Shape Human Progress*, Basic Books, 2000.

Harrison, Mark, "Coercion, Compliance, and the Collapse of the Soviet Command Economy," *Economic History Review*, Vol. 55, No. 3, August 2002.

Hay, Colin, "Crisis and the Structural Transformation of the State: Interrogating the Process of Change," *British Journal of Politics and International Relations*, Vol. 1, No. 3, October 1999.

Heffer, Simon, *High Minds: The Victorians and the Birth of Modern Britain*, Pegasus Books, 2022.

Heim, Jacob L., and Benjamin M. Miller, *Measuring Power, Power Cycles, and the Risk of Great-Power War in the 21st Century*, RAND Corporation, RR-2989-RC, 2020. As of June 1, 2023:
https://www.rand.org/pubs/research_reports/RR2989.html

Hellmuth, Eckhart, ed., *The Transformation of Political Culture: England and Germany in the Late Eighteenth Century*, Oxford University Press, 1990.

Hofstadter, Richard, *The Age of Reform: From Bryan to F.D.R.*, Knopf, 1955.

Hood, David Fredrick, "The Effects of the Cardwell Reforms on the British Victorian Army," California State University, Fresno, 2001.

Hoyer, Daniel, "Decline and Fall, Growth and Spread, or Resilience? Approaches to Studying How and Why Societies Change," pre-print of essay forthcoming in *Journal of World History*, SocArXiv, January 7, 2022.

Hoyer, Daniel, James S. Bennett, Harvey Whitehouse, Pieter François, Kevin Feeney, Jill Levine, Jenny Reddish, Donagh Davis, and Peter Turchin, "Flattening the Curve: Learning the Lessons of World History to Mitigate Societal Crises," SocArXiv, last updated July 19, 2022.

Hyma, Albert, "Calvinism and Capitalism in the Netherlands, 1555–1700," *Journal of Modern History*, Vol. 10, No. 3, September 1938.

Institute for Research on World-Systems, University of California, Riverside, "Last of the Hegemons," 2015. As of June 1, 2023:
https://irows.ucr.edu/papers/irows65/irows65.htm

Jacob, Margaret C., *The Cultural Meaning of the Scientific Revolution*, Temple University Press, 1988.

Kemp, Luke, "Diminishing Returns on Extraction," in Miguel A. Centeno, Peter W. Callahan, Paul A. Larcey, and Thayer S. Patterson, eds., *How Worlds Collapse: What History, Systems, and Complexity Can Teach About Our Modern World and Fragile Future*, Routledge, 2023.

Kennedy, Paul, *The Rise and Fall of Great Powers: Economic Change and Military Conflict from 1500 to 2000*, Vintage, 1989.

Khaldûn, Ibn, *The Muqaddimah: An Introduction to History – Abridged Edition*, ed. by N. J. Dawood, trans. by Franz Rosenthal, Princeton University Press, 2005.

Kidder, Tristram R., Liu Haiwang, Michael J. Storozum, and Qin Zhen, "New Perspectives on the Collapse and Regeneration of the Han Dynasty," in Ronald K. Faulseit, *Beyond Collapse: Archaeological Perspectives on Resilience, Revitalization, and Transformation in Complex Societies*, Southern Illinois University Press, 2016.

Kloppenberg, James T., *Uncertain Victory: Social Democracy and Progressivism in European and American Thought, 1870–1920*, Oxford University Press, 1986.

Kocher, Matthew Adam, "State Capacity as a Conceptual Variable," *Yale Journal of International Affairs*, Vol. 5, No. 2, 2010.

Kotkin, Stephen, *Armageddon Averted: The Soviet Collapse, 1970–2000*, Oxford University Press, 2001.

Kuru, Ahmet T., *Islam, Authoritarianism, and Underdevelopment: A Global and Historical Comparison*, Cambridge University Press, 2019.

Lears, Jackson, *Rebirth of a Nation: The Making of Modern America, 1877–1920*, HarperPerennial, 2010.

Levin, Michael, *The Condition of England Question: Carlyle, Mill, Engels*, St. Martin's Press, 1998.

Levy, Jack, *War in the Modern Great Power System: 1495–1975*, University Press of Kentucky, 1983.

Link, Arthur S., "What Happened to the Progressive Movement in the 1920's?" *American Historical Review*, Vol. 64, No. 4, 1959.

Lodge, George C., and Ezra F. Vogel, eds., *Ideology and National Competitiveness: An Analysis of Nine Countries*, Harvard Business School Press, 1987.

Mahdi, Muhsin, *Ibn Khaldûn's Philosophy of History: A Study in the Philosophic Foundation of the Science of Culture*, University of Chicago Press, 1964.

Mahmalat, Mounir, and Declan Curran, "Do Crises Induce Reform? A Critical Review of Conception, Methodology and Empirical Evidence of the 'Crisis Hypothesis,'" *Journal of Economic Surveys*, Vol. 32, No. 3, 2018.

Mazarr, Michael J., *The Societal Foundations of National Competitiveness*, RAND Corporation, RR-A499-1, 2022. As of June 1, 2023: https://www.rand.org/pubs/research_reports/RRA499-1.html

Mazarr, Michael J., Alexis Dale-Huang, and Matthew Sargent, *The Emerging Competitive Paradigm: A Contest of Effective Governance*, RAND Corporation, PE-A2611-1, February 2024. As of March 1, 2024: https://www.rand.org/pubs/perspectives/PEA2611-1.html

Mazarr, Michael J., Daniel Tapia, Anton Shenk, William Anthony Hay, Geoffrey Kabaservice, and Zongyuan Zoe Liu, *Public-Spirited Elites and National Fates*, RAND Corporation, RR-A2611-4, forthcoming.

McCraw, Thomas K., *Prophet of Innovation: Joseph Schumpeter and Creative Destruction*, Harvard University Press, 2007.

McDonald, Paul C., and Joseph M. Parent, *Twilight of the Titans: Great Power Decline and Retrenchment*, Cornell University Press, 2017.

McGerr, Michael E., *A Fierce Discontent: The Rise and Fall of the Progressive Movement in America, 1870–1920*, Free Press, 2003.

Miller, Chris, *The Struggle to Save the Soviet Economy: Mikhail Gorbachev and the Collapse of the USSR*, University of North Carolina Press, 2016.

Minford, Patrick, "Evaluating Mrs. Thatcher's Reforms: Britain's 1980s Economic Reform Program," in Francesco Giavazzi, Francesco Lefebvre D'Ovidio, and Alberto Mingardi, eds., *The Liberal Heart of Europe*, Palgrave Macmillan, 2021.

Mokyr, Joel, "The Intellectual Origins of Modern Economic Growth," *Journal of Economic History*, Vol. 65, No. 2, June 2005.

Mokyr, Joel, *A Culture of Growth: The Origins of the Modern Economy*, Princeton University Press, 2016.

National Research Council, *Disaster Resilience: A National Imperative*, National Academies Press, 2012.

Nove, Alec, "The Fall of Empires—Russia and the Soviet Union," in Geir Lundestad, ed., *The Fall of Great Powers: Peace, Stability, and Legitimacy*, Oxford University Press, 1994.

Nutt, Thomas, "Illegitimacy, Paternal Financial Responsibility, and the 1834 Poor Law Commission Report: The Myth of the Old Poor Law and the Making of the New," *Economic History Review*, Vol. 63, No. 2, 2010.

Ogilvie, Sheilagh, "State Capacity and Economic Growth: Cautionary Tales from History," *National Institute of Economic Review*, Vol. 262, No. 1, Autumn 2022, pp. 28–50.

Ohno, Kenichi, "Meiji Japan: Progressive Learning of Western Technology," in Arkebe Oqubay and Kenichi Ohno, eds., *How Nations Learn: Technological Learning, Industrial Policy, and Catch-Up*, Oxford University Press, 2019.

Olson, Mancur, *The Rise and Decline of Nations: Economic Growth, Stagflation, and Social Rigidities*, Yale University Press, 1982.

Organisation for Economic Co-operation and Development, "Level of GDP per Capita and Productivity," dataset, undated. As of September 19, 2023: https://stats.oecd.org/index.aspx?DataSetCode=PDB_LV

Our World in Data, "Data Page: Global GDP over the Long Run," from Max Roser, Pablo Arriagada, Joe Hasell, Hannah Ritchie, and Esteban Ortiz-Ospina, "Economic Growth," webpage, 2023. As of December 7, 2023: https://ourworldindata.org/grapher/global-gdp-over-the-long-run

Painter, Nell Irvin, *Standing at Armageddon: A Grassroots History of the Progressive Era*, W. W. Norton, 2008.

Plokhy, Serhii, "Chernobyl and the Fall of the Soviet Union," webpage, University of New South Wales, Centre for Ideas, undated. As of June 1, 2023: https://www.centreforideas.com/article/serhii-plokhy-chernobyl-and-fall-soviet-union

Plokhy, Serhii, *Chernobyl: The History of a Nuclear Catastrophe*, Basic Books, 2020.

Pomeranz, Kenneth, *The Great Divergence: China, Europe, and the Making of the World Economy*, Princeton University Press, 2000.

Pomeranz, Kenneth, "Calamities Without Collapse: Environment, Economy, and Society in China, ca. 1800–1949," in Patricia Ann McAnany and Norman Yoffee, eds., *Questioning Collapse: Human Resilience, Ecological Vulnerability, and the Aftermath of Empire*, Cambridge University Press, 2010.

Putnam, Robert D., *The Upswing: How America Came Together a Century Ago and How We Can Do It Again*, Simon and Schuster, 2022.

Ralston, Robert, "Make Us Great Again: The Causes of Declinism in Major Powers," *Security Studies*, Vol. 31, No. 4, 2022.

Rauch, Jonathan, *Demosclerosis*, Random House, 1994.

Reitan, Earl A., *The Thatcher Revolution: Margaret Thatcher, John Major, Tony Blair, and the Transformation of Modern Britain, 1979–2001*, Rowman & Littlefield Publishers, 2003.

Resolution Foundation and the Centre for Economic Performance, London School of Economics, *Ending Stagnation: A New Economic Strategy for Britain*, Resolution Foundation, December 2023.

Reuveny, Rafael, and Aseem Prakash, "The Afghanistan War and the Breakdown of the Soviet Union," *Review of International Studies*, Vol. 25, 1999.

Reynolds, Douglas B., "Soviet Economic Decline: Did an Oil Crisis Cause the Transition in the Soviet Union?" *Journal of Energy and Development*, Vol. 24, No. 1, 1998.

Roberts, David, "Tory Paternalism and Social Reform in Early Victorian England," *American Historical Review*, Vol. 63, No. 2, January 1958.

Rodgers, Daniel T., "In Search of Progressivism," *Reviews in American History*, Vol. 10, No. 4, 1982.

Rodgers, Daniel T., *Atlantic Crossings: Social Politics in a Progressive Age*, Harvard University Press, 2000.

Saunders, Robert, "The Politics of Reform and the Making of the Second Reform Act, 1848–1867," *Historical Journal*, Vol. 50, No. 3, September 2007.

Schama, Simon, *The Embarrassment of Riches: An Interpretation of Dutch Culture in the Golden Age*, Fontana Press, 1987.

Scheidel, Walter, *The Great Leveler: Violence and the History of Inequality from the Stone Age to the Twenty-First Century*, Princeton University Press, 2018.

Schwartz, Glenn M., and John J. Nichols, eds., *After Collapse: The Regeneration of Complex Societies*, University of Arizona Press, 2010.

Scott, Andrew M., "The Progressive Era in Perspective," *Journal of Politics*, Vol. 21, No. 4, 1959.

Sempa, Francis P., "Spengler, Toynbee, Burnham, and the Decline of the West," Russell Kirk Center, January 23, 2022.

Spengler, Oswald, *The Decline of the West*, George Allen & Unwin, 1926.

Steinbach, Susie L., *Understanding the Victorians: Politics, Culture, and Society in Nineteenth-Century Britain*, 3rd ed., Routledge Press, 2023.

Storey, Rebecca, and Glenn R. Storey, "Requestioning the Classic Maya Collapse and the Fall of the Roman Empire: Slow Collapse," in Robert K. Faulseit, ed., *Beyond Collapse: Archaeological Perspectives on Resilience, Revitalization, and Transformation in Complex Societies*, Center for Archaeological Investigations, Occasional Paper No. 42, 2016.

Tainter, Joseph A., "How Scholars Explain Collapse," in Miguel A. Centeno, Peter W. Callahan, Paul A. Larcey, and Thayer S. Patterson, eds., *How Worlds Collapse: What History, Systems, and Complexity Can Teach About Our Modern World and Fragile Future*, Routledge, 2023.

Taleb, Nassim Nicholas, *Antifragile: Things That Gain from Disorder*, Random House, 2012.

Taubman, William, *Gorbachev: His Life and Times*, Simon and Schuster, 2017.

Taylor, Miles, "Rethinking the Chartists: Searching for Synthesis in the Historiography of Chartism," *Historical Journal*, Vol. 39, No. 2, 1996.

Taylor, Miles, "Review: British Politics in the Age of Revolution and Reform, 1789–1867," *Historical Journal*, Vol. 45, No. 3, September 2002.

Thomas, James, "'Bound In by History': The Winter of Discontent in British Politics, 1979–2004," *Media, Culture & Society*, Vol. 29, No. 2, 2007.

Thompson, William R., "Dehio, Long Cycles, and the Geohistorical Context of Structural Transition," *World Politics*, Vol. 45, No. 1, 1992.

Toynbee, Arnold, *A Study of History*, Oxford University Press, 1934–1961.

U.S. Central Intelligence Agency, Office of Soviet Analysis, "USSR: Facing the Dilemma of Hard Currency Shortages," SOV 86-10027 X, May 1986, sanitized copy released December 1, 2011.

Van Reenen, John, "The Economic Legacy of Mrs. Thatcher Is a Mixed Bag," London School of Economics, April 10, 2013.

Wallerstein, Immanuel, "The Rise and Future Demise of the World Capitalist System: Concepts for Comparative Analysis," *Comparative Studies in Society and History*, Vol. 16, No. 4, September 1974.

Wallerstein, Immanuel, *World-Systems Analysis: An Introduction*, Duke University Press, 2004.

Ward, Steven, "Decline and Disintegration: National Status Loss and Domestic Conflict in Post-Disaster Spain," *International Security*, Vol. 46, No. 4, Spring 2022.

Watson, Peter, *The German Genius: Europe's Third Renaissance, the Second Scientific Revolution, and the Twentieth Century*, HarperCollins, 2010.

Watts, Stephen, Bryan Frederick, Jennifer Kavanagh, Angela O'Mahony, Thomas S. Szayna, Matthew Lane, Alexander Stephenson, and Colin P. Clarke, *A More Peaceful World? Regional Conflict Trends and U.S. Defense Planning*, RAND Corporation, RR-1177-A, 2017. As of June 1, 2023: https://www.rand.org/pubs/research_reports/RR1177.html

Weiss, Harvey, ed., *Megadrought and Collapse: From Early Agriculture to Angkor*, Oxford University Press, 2017.

Weisser, Henry, "Chartism in 1848: Reflections on a Non-Revolution," *Albion: A Quarterly Journal Concerned with British Studies* Vol. 13, No. 1, Spring 1981.

Wilson, A. N., *Prince Albert: The Man Who Saved the Monarchy*, Harper, 2019.

Winter, Alison, "Harriet Martineau and the Reform of the Invalid in Victorian England," *Historical Journal*, Vol. 38, No. 3, September 1995.

Zubok, Vladislav M., "The Collapse of the Soviet Union: Leadership, Elites, and Legitimacy," in Geir Lundestad, ed., *The Fall of Great Powers: Peace, Stability, and Legitimacy*, Oxford University Press, 1994.

Zubok, Vladislav M., *A Failed Empire: The Soviet Union in the Cold War from Stalin to Gorbachev*, University of North Carolina Press, 2007.